Y0-BSL-783

9 X 4/98 ✓ 8/01

DU BOIS

A Pictorial Biography

DU BOIS

A Pictorial Biography

by **Shirley Graham Du Bois**

 Johnson Publishing Company, Inc., Chicago, Illinois

First Edition

Copyright © (1978) by Estate of Shirley Graham Du Bois

Library of Congress Cataloging in Publication Data
Du Bois, Shirley Graham, 1906–1977.
Du Bois: a pictorial biography

1. Du Bois, William Edward Burghardt,
1868–1963—Biography—2.—Authors,
American—20th Century,—Biography

P.S. 3507.U 147Z 63   301.24'2'0924
77-16692
ISBN 0-87485-076-2

Designed by Norman L. Hunter
Printed in the United States of America

Acknowledgements

GRATEFUL acknowledgement is extended to the University of Massachusetts at Andover for their gracious permission to use the many photographs from the special collection of W. E. B. Du Bois material in their archives. We are particularly grateful to Mrs. Katherine Emerson, Archivist at the University, for her assistance and kind forbearance during the lengthy period of the project's preparation.

We are also grateful to the University of Massachusetts Press for permission to use a number of photographs, previously published in their volumes of the Correspondence of W. E. B. Du Bois: Volume I, Selections, 1877–1934 (1973) and Volume II, Selections, 1934–1944 (1976). We must thank also Sidney Myers, Legal Counsel to the Chancellor of the University of Massachusetts, Andover, for his assistance and advice.

To Moses Asch and Folkways Records and Service Corporation, our gratitude for permission to use quotations from the recording, The Autobiography of W. E. B. Du Bois.

To The Crisis Magazine and the National Association for the Advancement of Colored People for permission to reprint, "so the girl marries," Crisis, our thanks.

The Gordon Parks photos of W. E. B. Du Bois are courtesy of EBONY magazine.

We are deeply indebted to David Graham Du Bois for his patience and for the moving and sensitive foreword to this book.

Our thanks and deep appreciation to Bernard Jaffe, Esq., long-time friend, confidant and attorney for Mrs. Shirley Graham Du Bois. His advice, counsel, encouragement and permission to make liberal use of material published in Mrs. Du Bois' earlier work, *His Day Is Marching On* (Lippincott) made it possible to complete the fleshing out of skeletal references to incidents in the author's own words.

Sincere thanks to Lerone Bennett, Jr. for the introduction written at the personal request of Shirley Graham Du Bois upon the occasion of her last visit to Chicago and the day she signed the contract for the Pictorial Biography of W. E. B. Du Bois.

My thanks to Basil O. Phillips, photo editor, for his patience in assisting in the search for elusive photographs, and for the tedious business of handling old and fragile originals with understanding care.

To Norman L. Hunter, art director and designer, whose commitment to this project was unfailing, I am eternally grateful. To Jerry Dibblee, account executive at Rand McNally, who helped to guide us through the maze, in order that the final product would be the kind of book that Shirley Graham Du Bois envisioned, my deep and profound thanks.

To Rose Jourdain Hayes, who supplied the photo of her grandfather, E. B. Jourdain, one of the original "29" in the Niagara Movement, our thanks.

To Mrs. Elizabeth Moos, who supplied slides of the European trip for Mrs. Du Bois' use in the photographic memoir, we are grateful.

And to Mr. John H. Johnson, publisher, whose vision and foresight and patience, in the final analysis made this project a reality.

Doris E. Saunders
Editor

Foreword

MY mother's enthusiasm and delight at the prospect of Johnson Publishing Company producing a pictorial biography of Dr. W. E. B. Du Bois was so great she uncharacteristically refused to inform her long-time friend, confidant and personal lawyer, Bernard Jaffe, until after she had signed the contract. She told me later that she feared his white, Madison Avenue-lawyer image would jeopardize the project. She felt strongly that a Johnson-published book on Dr. Du Bois would ultimately find its way into far more Afro-American homes than one done by any major, white-owned publishing house. This is what she passionately wanted. She was not going to allow wrangling over terms to interfere. She was confident that Johnson Publishing Company would do a book worthy of its illustrious subject. She could not imagine anything else.

The first entry in the journal my mother kept through the last year of her life includes a revealing expression of concern about her commitment to Johnson Publishing Company, made just weeks before she left the U.S.A. for treatment in China. Warned by her doctors that delaying hospitalization was extremely inadvisable, she nevertheless insisted upon a two-week layover in Cairo, Egypt (her home since 1967), in order to fulfill that commitment. Weak and in pain—and we now know already hopelessly riddled with cancer—she completed that commitment: the selection and captioning of additional photos from her vast collection in Cairo and the preparation of textual materials.

On February 23, 1976, the day my mother was admitted to Peking's Capitol Hospital, by mere chance Dr. Du Bois' birthday, and, 13 months before her death, my mother began her daily journal of that extraordinary year. Looking back she wrote:

> "Preparations to leave the United States and start my Long Journey, questions of how I could carry out my commitments to Johnson Publishing Company for the pictorial biography of W. E. B.,

telling dear friends 'good-bye' without making the good-byes too final, struggling against pain—all combined to prevent my starting this diary with contemplated phrases on 'resignation' and 'facing death with calm nobility.' Facing life was my immediate problem, which fact wiped out philosophical phrase-making . . ."

And, face life she did. Never once during that torturous final year did my mother express doubt of her ultimate recovery. This volume is my mother's last completed literary creation. It is a major contribution to the legacy left us by Dr. W. E. B. Du Bois and a fitting conclusion and memorial to the life of Shirley Graham Du Bois, whose later years were so totally devoted to promoting and safe-guarding that legacy; whose whole life, like that of Dr. Du Bois, was uncompromisingly committed to the liberation of humankind, particularly peoples of color, from all forms of racism, exploitation, and oppression.

David Graham Du Bois

October 1, 1977
Cairo, Egypt

Introduction

WHEN he died at 10:40 on Tuesday night, August 27, 1963, the *Ghanaian Times* printed a bold black headline:

THIS DAY A MIGHTY TREE HAS FALLEN IN AFRICA

This a photographic essay on one of the tallest trees of Africa and African-America—a photographic essay on the roots, the development, trials, tribulations, joys, and triumphs of W. E. B. Du Bois, who was an American original and one of the largest minds produced on this land. Large in life, larger even in death, Du Bois left a challenging legacy.

He was a founder of the NAACP, and he almost singlehandedly created the modern black protest movement and the Pan-African movement. More importantly perhaps, he was, as I said in *Pioneers in Protest*, the discoverer of the New World of Africa and of African-America. He was perhaps the first black man to see the shores beyond the Europeanized West. He was perhaps the first black man to proclaim, with all his heart and with all his soul, the dusk of dawn of the Third World. Black Power, *Negritude*, the African personality, Africa for Africans, the sociology of the slums, the *Gift of Black Folk*, the *Souls of Black Folk*, the *Dusk of Dawn*: all found a place in the worldview of the prophet who said in 1903: "The problem of the twentieth century is the problem of the color-line—the relation of the darker to the lighter races of men in Asia and Africa, in America and the islands of the sea."

In 1934, the Board of Directors of the NAACP said that "the ideas which he propounded in *The Crisis* and in his books and essays transformed the Negro World as well as a large portion of the liberal white world, so that the whole problem of the relation of black and white races has ever since had a completely new orientation. He created, what never existed before, a Negro intelligentsia, and many who have never read a word of his writings are his spiritual disciples and descendants . . . ."

Du Bois studied history and acted in history. But he also embodied history in the flesh. He was one month old when Ulysses Grant became

President, eight years old when Victoria became Empress of India, nine when white men with guns nullified Reconstruction, sixty-two when Gandhi marched to the sea, and ninety-five when he died on the eve of the great March on Washington.

The story of this singular adventure of our culture has been told many times. But the collection of rare and revealing photographs assembled here by his second wife, Shirley Graham Du Bois, gives a new dimension to his personal adventure. And so what we have here is a photographic meditation on history, on the life, the styles, the clothing, the *textures* of whole periods. Here are new and exciting photographs of the forgotten dreamers and protesters of the nineteenth and twentieth centuries. Here are invaluable behind-the-scenes portraits of the great and near-great of the world. Here also are new images of Du Bois the man. The photograph of Mao Tse-Tung and Du Bois, laughing, as Shirley Du Bois said, "like two schoolboys," is worth the price of the book alone.

This book was the last testament of Shirley Du Bois who worked on it, with loving attention to detail, until her illness and untimely death in March, 1977. It is a valuable addition to the Du Bois bibliography. It is also a moving and challenging testament to the indomitable tenacity of the human spirit as embodied in the lives of two great witnesses of the Dawn—Shirley Graham Du Bois and William Edward Burghardt Du Bois.

Lerone Bennett, Jr.
Chicago, December, 1977

Contents

William E. B. Du Bois and Shirley Graham Du Bois

Du Bois

A Pictorial Biography

W. E. B. Du Bois in his mother's arms, Spring, 1868. He said, "My mother was brown and rather small with smooth skin and lovely eyes, and hair that curled and crinkled down each side of her forehead from the part in the middle. She was rather silent, but very determined and very patient."

Du Bois

A Pictorial Biography

Part One

ARY Sylvina Burghardt, Du Bois' mother, was born in the Housatonic Valley of western Massachusetts. The black Burghardts were a group of African-Americans descended from Tom, who was born in West Africa about 1730. He was stolen by Dutch slave traders and brought to the valley of the Hudson as a small child. He grew up in the service of the Burghardts, a white family of Dutch descent. Early in the 18th century the Burghardts moved east from the Hudson Valley and settled in Berkshire County of what is now Massachusetts. The country was described then as a "howling wilderness."

When the Revolutionary War broke out, Tom Burghardt appeared with the rank of private on the muster and payroll of the Berkshire County Regiment. When the war was won, Tom and his family were given land on the South Egremont Plain, as a result of his war service.

Here during the late 18th and early 19th centuries a clan of free blacks developed, tending their farms and preserving African traditions. "They spread slowly through the country, intermarrying among cousins and other black folk," according to Du Bois, "with some, but limited infiltration of white blood and . . . some intermingling with local Indians."

Tom's son, Jack Burghardt, had several children, one of whom was Othello, Du Bois' grandfather. Othello and his wife Sally Lampman were both born slaves, but freed, at their majority according to Massachusetts law. They were the parents of Mary Sylvina, Du Bois' mother. She was born at Great Barrington, Massachusetts, January 14, 1831 and died there in 1885 at the age of 54.

Alfred Du Bois, a light mulatto, was Du Bois' father. He came to Great Barrington shortly after the Civil War, met and married Mary Sylvina Burghardt.

In the early 17th century, two French Huguenots, Jacques and Louis Du Bois, sons of Chretien Du Bois of Wicres, near Lille, in French Flanders, migrated to America. Perhaps it was to escape religious persecution. Jacques had stopped off in Leiden in the Netherlands, and he brought with him his French-Dutch family. They settled at Kingston, New York. One of his children was James Du Bois. According to the written testimony of Alexander Du Bois (a son of James), his father was a physician and a landholder along the Hudson and in the Bahama islands, and was W. E. B. Du Bois' paternal great-grandfather.

Dr. James Du Bois never married, but one of his Bahamian slave women was his common-law wife. They had two sons, Alexander and John. Alexander and John were brought by their father to the United States about 1810. Their mother was dead. The two fair-skinned sons were entered in an Episcopal boys' school at Cheshire, Connecticut. Their father, Dr. James Du Bois, visited them regularly until he died suddenly of a stroke about 1812.

Dr. Du Bois left no will, so his estate went to a cousin. His sons Alexander and John were left penniless black orphans. They were taken out of school and bound out as apprentices by their white uncle; Alexander to a shoemaker, and the whereabouts of John Du Bois became lost. Alexander Du Bois married Sarah Marsh Lewis in 1823 and emigrated to Haiti where two children, Augusta and Alfred, were born. The Haitian climate did not agree with Sarah Du Bois, and she died, leaving Alexander with two children to raise. He returned to the United States and very shortly married Emily Basset Jacklyn, a widow, in New Milford, Connecticut.

Alfred Du Bois, W. E. B.'s father, shown in his Union Army uniform. A volunteer in the 54th Massachusetts regiment, he was small, olive-skinned and just visibly colored, with curly hair.

4

For a time Alexander Du Bois worked as a steward on the New York–New Haven boat; later he operated a grocery store in New Haven. In 1847 he helped to form New Haven's Episcopal Parish of St. Luke (for Colored). Alexander Du Bois served St. Luke's as senior warden for many years.

Alexander Du Bois and his son Alfred did not get along well. Alexander Du Bois was a formal man, and his son was, according to Du Bois, "gay and carefree, refusing to settle long at any one place or job. He was a barber, a merchant, and a preacher, but always irresponsible and charming. He wandered from eastern New England where his father lived and came to the Berkshire valley in 1867, where he met and married my brown mother." Du Bois' father was then forty-two and his mother thirty-six years old.

He said of his family, "My immediate family consisted of a very dark grandfather, Othello Burghardt, sitting beside the fireplace in a high chair because of an injured hip. He was good-natured but not energetic. The energy was in my grandmother, Sarah Lampman, "Sally," a thin, tall, yellow and hawk-faced woman . . . beautiful in her youth and efficient and managing in her age. . . . For a time I lived in the country at the house of my grandfather, Othello, one of three farming brothers. . . . My father's father, Alexander Du Bois, lived in New Bedford. A short, thick-set man, he was hard and set in his ways, proud and bitter. I went to New Bedford in 1883 at the age 15. . . . My skin was darker than that of my schoolmates. My family confined itself not entirely but largely to people of this same darker hue."

Small Willie Du Bois early in 1872. He was furious when mistaken for a little girl and cried until his mother cut his curls off.

Education was not uncommon in Du Bois' family. He said, "For several generations my people had attended schools for longer or shorter periods, so most of them could read and write. I was brought up from my earliest years with the idea of regular attendance at school. I started on one school ground . . . at the age of five or six and continued there until I was graduated from high school at sixteen. . . . The curriculum was simple—reading, writing, spelling and arithmetic, grammar, geography and history. We learned the alphabet; we were drilled rigorously on the multiplication table and we drew accurate maps. We could spell correctly and read clearly."

Through the church people in Great Barrington, Du Bois was given a scholarship to Fisk University in Nashville, Tennessee. He entered as a sophomore in the fall of 1885. His mother died just before he left for college. It was a totally new experience for him, being in a segregated world. For the first time he heard Negro spirituals. He was sure he had never seen such beautiful people nor heard such beautiful music. Du Bois took a leadership role from the beginning and worked in various capacities on the staff of the *Fisk Herald*.

The summer of his junior year, Du Bois taught in the back-country schools of rural Tennessee, and out of his experience grew some of his most memorable essays. He described the Fisk experience, "I went from my home in Massachusetts when I was 17 down to Fisk University in Tennessee. There I stayed three years. At Fisk we had an institution for Negroes—taught for the most part by white people who were graduates of Oberlin and Yale. The College was after the New England tradition. The regular College was Latin and Greek and mathematics and history . . . comparatively small classes, because in the whole College Department there were only about 25 very good teachers. The general surroundings *inside* the College were excellent. I think that my long years of life are due perhaps to one thing that I learned at Fisk and that was to go to bed at 10:00 at night.

Then, of course, there was what was to me, the new experience of being with my own group of people. In New England I was usually the one colored pupil with surrounding white pupils. It was not until I began to get along in the teens that I felt any differences, and there the differences were comparatively small. And yet, as I look back I can see that probably I felt myself to be the exception.

When Du Bois graduated from Great Barrington High School (Mass.) in 1884, he was the youngest and only non-white member of the class. He delivered the commencement oration.

9

On the other hand, I go down to Fisk University and suddenly I am in a Negro world, where all the people, except the teachers (and the teachers too, in thought and action), belong to this colored world, and the world was almost complete. We acted and thought as people belonging to this group, and I got the idea that my work was in that group. While I was, in the long run, going to try to break down segregation and separateness, for the time I was quite willing to be a Negro and to work within a Negro group."

In 1887, his senior year, he was made editor-in-chief of the *Fisk Herald*. He organized a glee club of male students, and following graduation in June 1888, they earned money working and singing in hotels.

After Du Bois graduated from Fisk University in 1888, he applied for and was given the Price-Greenleaf Aid of $300 to attend Harvard University. He entered in the junior class in the fall of 1888. It brought him back to Massachusetts and to the greater Boston community. He recalled: "Now, of course, in Boston there were colored people. There were some colored students in other institutions (in 1892 Du Bois and Clement Morgan attended the Amherst graduation of George W. Forbes, William T. Jackson and William H. Lewis). There were only a few colored students at Harvard, one or two besides myself during my whole terms there. But there were colored people in Massachusetts, and I had a very pleasant social life with them so I was not lonely at all and I enjoyed the life there.

"Then too, Harvard was in an exceptional state of being at that time. I do not think that from 1885 to this day, there has been quite an aggregation of teachers and preachers and lecturers as there were then. My closest friend, for instance, as a teacher, was William James, the great sociologist, brother of Henry James. I knew him well; I was invited to his house and we talked together. Then there was George Santayana. He and I read the *Kritik der Reinen Vernuft* together, alone up in an attic room. There was (William Ellery) Channing, the historian; and many of the greater names in history were connected more or less with the institution.

Du Bois entered Fisk in fall of 1885. For the first time he was in a community of dark-skinned people like himself. For the first time he heard Negro spirituals. He was sure he had never seen such beautiful people nor heard such beautiful music. The Fisk Faculty in the years 1885–88 was headed by Reverend Erastus Milo Cravath, President. Professor William Morris and Mrs. Lucy Green were favorite teachers. Du Bois wrote on the *Fisk Herald* and organized a small glee club of male students. During the summer of 1888 they earned money working and singing in resort hotels. He graduated in the class of 1888. Du Bois is seated at left in photo above.

11

"I had always thought as a boy, that I was going to Harvard.

"When I went to Harvard, I had made up my mind that I was going to study philosophy. That is, I wanted to study the thought of what *was* the meaning of the whole universe. Coming from Fisk to Harvard was a change, and yet, I met it in a peculiar sort of way. If I had gone directly from my high school in Great Barrington to Harvard, I would have thought of myself as a Massachusetts man and my fellows would have been the whites there. But, coming from Fisk I brought with me the feeling of a separate race.

"I never felt myself to be a Harvard man as I had felt myself a Fisk man. I was coming to Harvard for a particular purpose—to try to further the education that I had received at Fisk, to work by myself, and to seek no contact with my fellows. If they wanted to know me, the effort would have to be on their part. Out of a class of 300, I don't suppose that I knew ten really, intimately at all.

"After I got there and had studied one or two years under James, we had a frank talk. James said, 'No if you have to study philosophy, you will, but if you can get out of it, you had better because it is difficult to make a living at philosophy.' So I gave up philosophy and went into history under Albert Bushnell Hart. I had some assignments in Negro history, and was very interested in the work that I was doing; it was work that Hart particularly wanted done. Eventually, I took several courses for my broader education; courses in chemistry, mathematics, and geology, and then finally began to concentrate on history, especially the history of the Negro in the United States and later in Africa.

"I received my bachelor's degree from Harvard with distinction in 1890; I was one of the six Commencement speakers out of my class of 300. I took as my subject, Jefferson Davis, as a representative of civilization. I tried to be very fair and frank in discussing the kind of civilization that he represented—the might of the white race oppressing the rest of the world, which was a thing that we did not need and would not want in the next century. It proved a rather popular subject and there was a good deal of talk about it.

"I applied for a graduate fellowship and got one for a year. In the midst of that year, I was at a party and somebody called my attention to what Rutherford B. Hayes, ex-President of the U.S., had said at Johns Hopkins. (I have said that at Harvard they were trying to keep the New England aristocrats from running the whole thing. In my class was a black man from St. Louis who was one of the best speakers and one of the best users of English that I ever knew, Clement Morgan. At Harvard, when it came to the election of class officers, they were always Lowells and Cabots and Saltonstalls, and so forth. The class revolted and elected Morgan as the class orator, which was unprecedented. They talked about it all over the U.S.)

"At that time, Rutherford B. Hayes was head of the Slater Fund, which was based on money left by a Connecticut millionnaire to educate Negroes, but Hayes said they had only been able to find orators. Well, I got angry at that, and I wrote Mr. Hayes and told him that I could get some professors to tell him that I was doing pretty good work, and that I should like to study in Germany. That was at the time when every American who wanted to get a real position in a University had to go to Germany to get his degree.

"Mr. Hayes wrote back politely and said that the Fund had offered some money for scholarships for Negroes, but that they were not being offered then. Following this, I wrote him a pretty impudent letter and said that he owed somebody an apology. He had no business going down to a southern university and speaking about a scholarship being offered, but not being able to find anybody. As matter of fact, I had never heard of any such scholarships being offered, and I could not find out from any one else that they had heard. Well, Mr. Hayes wrote a very apologetic letter and said that he was sorry and would take up the matter the very next year, if I wished. The next year, I started on him again, and I got everybody from the President of Harvard on down, to write. He was simply overwhelmed with recommendations. I got a fellowship. Meanwhile, I had gotten a renewal on my fellowship, so that I spent two years in the Harvard Graduate School. Then I got the fellowship to Germany. It was $750, half of it was a gift and half was to be paid back after I had finished my education. I eventually paid it back with interest at 6 percent."

Du Bois in group of commencement speakers in the graduating class of 281 seniors from Harvard in 1890. Du Bois graduated *cum laude* in philosophy. The subject of his commencement address was "Jefferson Davis." "I wanted," he explained, "to consider not the man, but the type of civilization which his life represented: its foundation—the idea of the strong man—the rule of might." A Harvard professor wrote to *Kate Field's Washington,* then an important periodical: "Du Bois, the colored orator of the commencement made a ten-strike. It is agreed upon by all I have seen that he was star of the occasion. One of the trustees of the University told me that his paper was considered masterly in every way."

After taking his Master's degree from Harvard, in the fall of 1892, Du Bois entered the University of Berlin in Germany. Photo shows him with large group of Berlin University students.

Du Bois went to Germany for advanced study. As he has said, "There I had a tremendous new experience. For the first time in my life, I was just a human being and not a particular kind of human being.

"In Berlin I had the chance to get into a seminar, which was rather unusual for a foreigner, but I was allowed in this seminar on economics under two of the most prominent professors. I wanted to take the examination, but the rule was that you could not come up for an examination until you had been three semesters at the university, and I had only been two, because I only had money for two. They tried to make an exception, but the English professor had a lot of candidates, so that no difference could be made. I brought to their attention the fact that I had already had two years at Harvard, but they did not recognize Harvard as being of the same rank as Berlin. So I had to come back without my degree. On the other hand, it is rather interesting to know that in *1958*, when I was in Berlin, the university brought out my records and gave me the degree that I did not get some 70 years before."

Part Two

Du BOIS was 26 when he returned from his two years in Germany in 1894. He began his search for a teaching post at a Black college by sending out letters. His first offer came from Wilberforce University where he was offered the classics chair and a salary of eight hundred dollars a year. He also received an offer from Lincoln Institute in Missouri with a salary of one thousand and fifty dollars a year. Last, he received, by telegram, the following offer, "Can give mathematics if terms suit. Will you accept? Booker T. Washington." It is interesting to speculate what changes might have been wrought in the history of the next score of years had Du Bois accepted the Washington offer instead of going to the AME church school in Ohio, Wilberforce.

Wilberforce was a small college with a proud tradition in African Methodism. Du Bois said many times that it was a bit incongruous, the picture of him with cane and gloves from his German student life, and his ideas of what a university should be shaped by his years at Harvard and in Berlin.

Photographs of Wilberforce faculty, staff, and students during Du Bois tenure. He is standing, derby in hand, in top row at far right.

20

21

He told an amusing story of wandering into chapel shortly after his arrival on the Wilberforce campus. The student leader of the chapel service announced that, "Professor Du Bois will lead us in prayer." To which Du Bois replied, "No, he won't." He said that it took a lot of explaining to the Board of Bishops to make them understand that Professor Du Bois, or any other teacher on their payroll, could not and would not lead students in prayer at a chapel service.

He remained at Wilberforce for two years. During that time he met Nina Gomer, a young student from Cedar Rapids, Iowa. To her Du Bois must have seemed much like Prince Charming from another world. A slender, quiet, darkeyed girl, Nina's mother was a native of Alsace in France and her father, a chef in Cedar Rapids' leading hotel.

At the end of two years at Wilberforce he and Nina were married. He took her with him to Philadelphia where he had been offered a temporary appointment for one year at the University of Pennsylvania as "assistant instructor." He was paid $600 for the year, but the money was less important to him than the opportunity to design a social science research project based on scientifically structured investigation. His study of the Black community in Philadelphia has withstood the test of time and is even today looked upon as a model for the social scientist.

Nina remained with him at their simple home in the Philadelphia slums until shortly before the birth of their first child. Then Du Bois took her to the Burghardt's in Great Barrington. Here their infant son, Burghardt, was born.

The title page of the monumental sociological study, *The Philadelphia Negro*, published in 1899.

Publications

OF THE

University of Pennsylvania

—

SERIES IN

Political Economy and Public Law

———

NO. 14

THE PHILADELPHIA NEGRO

A SOCIAL STUDY

———

BY

W. E. BURGHARDT DU BOIS, Ph. D.

Some time Assistant in Sociology in the University of Pennsylvania; Professor
of Economics and History in Atlanta University; Author of
" The Suppression of the African Slave-Trade."

TOGETHER WITH

A SPECIAL REPORT ON DOMESTIC SERVICE

BY

ISABEL EATON, A. M.

Fellow of the College Settlements' Association

———

Published for the University

PHILADELPHIA

1899

GINN & CO., Selling Agents, Tremont Place, Boston, Mass.

He wrote touchingly of the experience of fatherhood in *Souls of Black Folk:*

What is this tiny formless thing, this newborn wail from an unknown world,—all head and voice? I handle it curiously, and watch perplexed its winking breathing, and sneezing. I did not love it then; it seemed a ludicrous thing to love; but her I loved, my girl-mother, she whom I now saw unfolding like the glory of the morning—the transfigured woman. Through her I came to love the wee thing, as it grew and waxed strong; as its little soul unfolded itself in twitter and cry and half-formed word, and as its eyes caught the gleam and flash of life. How beautiful he was, with his olive-tinted flesh and dark gold ringlets, his eyes of mingled blue and brown, his perfect little limbs, and the soft voluptuous roll which the blood of Africa had moulded into his features!...

So sturdy and masterful he grew, so filled with bubbling life, so tremulous with the unspoken wisdom of a life but eighteen months distant from the All-life,—we were not far from worshipping this revelation of the divine, my wife and I....

By now Nina Du Bois and the baby were living on the campus of Atlanta University where he had been invited by President Horace Bum-

Du Bois' first wife, Nina Gomer, whom he married while teaching at Wilberforce University in Xenia, Ohio, 1896. The baby is the first child, Burghardt, born in Great Barrington, Massachusetts in 1898. The photographs were made in Atlanta, Georgia, where Du Bois was teaching at Atlanta University. At the left, Burghardt is two and a half months old, and in the other two he is eight months old. The little boy died at eighteen months. His death evoked Du Bois' most poignant piece of writing: "Of the Passing of the First Born" in *Souls of Black Folk*.

stead to develop a department of sociology and to direct a series of conferences on the American Negro.

Here with their little son they were happy, until that awful time he has recounted in *Passing of the First Born.*

One night the little feet pattered wearily to the wee white bed, and the tiny hands trembled; and a warm flushed face tossed on the pillow. . . . Ten days he lay there,—a swift week and three endless days, . . . wasting away. . . . He died at eventide, when the sun lay like a brooding sorrow above the western hills, veiling its face; when the winds spoke not, and the trees, the great green trees he loved, stood motionless. I saw his breath beat quicker and quicker, pause, and then his little soul leapt like a star that travels in the night and left a world of darkness in its train. The day changed not; the same tall trees peeped in at the windows, the same green grass glinted in the setting sun. Only in the chamber of death writhed the world's most piteous thing—a childless mother. . . . We could not lay him in the ground there in Georgia, for the earth there is strangely red; so we bore him away to the northward, with his flowers and his little folded hands. . . . All that day and all that night there sat an awful gladness in my heart, . . . and my soul whispers ever to me, saying, "Not dead, not dead, but escaped; not bound, but free." No bitter meanness now shall sicken his baby heart till it die a living death, no taunt shall madden his happy boyhood. . . . In the poise of his little curl-crowned head did there not sit all that wild pride of being which his father had hardly crushed in his own heart? For what, forsooth, shall a Negro want with pride among the studied humiliations of fifty million fellows? Well sped, my boy, before the world has dubbed your ambition insolence, has held your ideals unattainable, and taught you to cringe and bow. Better far this nameless void that stops my life than a sea of sorrow for you.*

After the death of little Burghardt, Nina seemed to shrink more and more into herself. The birth of a daughter, Nina Yolande, sixteen months later, did not restore the girlish smile or bring consolation. She grieved ever after for her little boy.

---

* Excerpted from "Of the Passing of the First-Born," *Souls of Black Folk*, A. C. McClurg and Co., 1903.

Part Three

Du BOIS said of the 13 years that he spent at Atlanta University, and of the ten-year cycle of published studies that covered every aspect of the American Negro's life, "For the next twenty-five years there wasn't a book published on the Negro problem that didn't have to depend upon what we were doing at Atlanta University. Ours was the first institution in the United States, white or black, that had any course on the history of the American Negro or on Negro history in general."

But it was while he was at Atlanta that his faith in knowledge as a solution to the problem of race was shaken. *The Souls of Black Folk,* a collection of his essays, was published in 1903. One of them, *Of Mr. Booker T. Washington and Others,* was highly critical of the Tuskeegee educator. He said, "It wasn't enough to teach Negroes trades . . . Negroes had to have some voice in their government, they had to have some protection in the courts, they had to have trained men to lead them."

In 1905, Du Bois sent out the summons for the gathering which came to be known as the Niagara Movement. Accommodations for the meeting could not be found in Buffalo, New York, therefore it was held in a small hotel on the Canadian side of the falls at Port Erie.

P. NADAR   PARIS

CARTE D'EXPOSANT.

1900.

Signature du titulaire:

W. E. B DuBois

Du Bois arranged a display on American Blacks for the Paris Exhibition of 1900. His collection took the bronze medal. Shown in tails and top hat on the way to afternoon reception. It was his first trip to Europe since his student days. Top left, W. E. B.'s identification card for the Paris Exposition. Pan-African idea was born.

Du Bois, above, in his office at Atlanta University, circa 1909. He was nearing the decision to leave Atlanta to join the NAACP, and was greatly concerned over the future of *The Horizon*, the news organ of the Niagara Movement. As it turned out, *The Crisis* took over the subscription list of *The Horizon* and Du Bois continued editing a journal "of opinion."

Atlanta University staff and faculty with children in 1906. Young Yolande Du Bois is in front row, Nina Gomer Du Bois, center, and Du Bois right rear. Above, Du Bois with colleagues at Atlanta University.

The National Negro Business League was organized in Boston in August, 1900, by Booker T. Washington to bring together a group of successful business people as an organized base of support for Washington's program of economic progress as opposed to political involvement. In the early days Du Bois was still trying to effect an accord with Washington, and, in fact, had praised the business group in *Souls of Black Folk*. Others in photo are J. C. Napier, Fred R. Moore and Emmett Scott.

Twenty-nine men from fourteen states attended the founding meeting of the Niagara Movement in 1905. Fifty-nine black men from seventeen different states had signed a call for a meeting in Buffalo. The Movement was incorporated January 31, 1906. Right, E. B. Jourdain, from Massachusetts, and George W. Mitchell, of Pennsylvania (not pictured), were among the founders.

"The Original Twenty-nine."

Second meeting of the Niagara Movement was at Harper's Ferry, W. Va. in 1906. At a sunrise gathering, John Brown, one of Du Bois' heroes, was eulogized for his efforts to free the slaves. Brown was also the subject of an impassioned biography by Du Bois published in 1909 by George W. Jacobs and Company. Shown above, J. L. Clifford, L. M. Hershaw, F. H. M. Murray and W. E. B. Du Bois at Harper's Ferry Conference.

William Monroe Trotter, also a Harvard man, was an outspoken critic of Washington. He edited and published the *Guardian*, a weekly newspaper in Boston. J. Max Barber, another Niagara man, was editor of *The Voice of the Negro*, an Atlanta based magazine, which provided a needed outlet for Du Bois and the Niagara Movement. After the Atlanta riot, Barber was forced to leave Atlanta and publication of *The Voice of the Negro* soon ceased. Much of the Black Press was under the direct influence of Booker T. Washington during this period. Charles Bentley and James Madden, the two Chicagoans who attended the Niagara organization meeting, were local leaders in the integration movement. Frederick McGhee, one of the most stalwart backers of the Niagara Movement, was a Minneapolis attorney. Almost all qualified as members of the Talented Tenth, the segment of the colored population that Du Bois felt must accept the responsibility for leadership of the masses. Below: group of 45 of the members of Niagara Movement present at Harper's Ferry. Bottom Row, Reading Left to Right—F. H. Murray, Va.; Dr. O. M. Waller, N.Y.; Rev. G. R. Waller, Md.; W. D. Johnson, Mass.; Dr. C. E. Bentley, Ill.; J. R. Clifford, W. Va.; Prof. W. E. B. Du Bois, Ga.; Rev. B. Gunner, R.I.; G. W. Mitchell, Esq., Penn.; C. G. Morgan, Mass.; L. M. Hershaw, D.C. Second Row—T. M. Dent, D.C.; Lt. J. C. Andrews, Mass.; Rev. O. L. Mitchell, D.C.; Rev. G. F. Miller, N.Y.; Chas. A. King, Mass.; Prof. M. A. Hawkins, Md.; Prof. John Hope, Ga.; F. L. McGhee, Esq., Minn.; J. Max Barber, Ga.; Capt. H. A. Thompson, N.Y.; W. J. Carter, Esq., Penn.; W. Monroe Trotter, Mass.; G. W. Crawford, Esq., Conn.; Dr. H. E. Young, Md.; Rev. J. M. Waldron, Fla.; Rev. G. F. Bragg, Md.; Rev. W. Bishop Johnson, D.C.; Rev. S. E. Griggs, Tenn. Third Row—Rev. J. T. Brown, D.C.; Rev. R. C. Ransom, Mass.; F. S. Monroe, Mass.; Dr. H. L. Bailey, D.C.; W. A. Hawkins, Md.; Prof. J. W. Barco, Va.; Rev. Robt. W. Goff, Va.; J. B. Watson, Ga.; Prof. C. L. Davis, Md.; A. S. Gray, D.C.; Prof. W. A. Rogers, Va.; T. A. Johnson, D.C. Top row in windows of Anthony Hall—Prof. H. T. Pratt, Md.; Jno. Hurst, Md.; Rev. H. C. Garner, D.C.; J. C. Stewart, D.C.

38

Du Bois and Clement G. Morgan, Harvard classmate, are seated in front of delegates to Niagara Movement Meeting at Faneuil Hall, Boston, 1907.

Twenty-nine men from fourteen states attended the founding meeting. At the end, a Declaration of Principals was issued, which covered the wide range of Black protest against lynch law, denial of the ballot, segregation of facilities, inadequate schools and housing, unemployment, and peonage. By 1906, the Niagara Movement was labeled "radical." They met that year at Harper's Ferry, the scene of John Brown's martyrdom. 1906 was also the terrible year of the Atlanta Riots. Du Bois was out of town on a speaking engagement, but when he returned he wrote *Litany for Atlanta.* After the 1907 meeting in Boston, the Niagara Movement lost its momentum.

In conjunction with L. M. Hershaw and F. H. M. Murray, Du Bois published, from 1907 to 1910, a small magazine called *The Horizon.* It served as something of an organ for the intellectuals who had been a part of the Niagara Movement. *The Horizon* ceased publication when *The Crisis* was born in the fall of 1910.

Du Bois increased visibility as the leader of this "radical Northern" movement made his continued association with a Southern Negro college difficult. He said, "The people who were supporting Atlanta University were a little uneasy about the way in which I talked about the Negro problem and the pressure began to be put upon the University to do without my services." He recalled, "At last I resigned. They would have had to drop me if they wanted to keep the philanthropic gifts coming from the rich people of the North." Du Bois spent 13 years at Atlanta University and made an invaluable contribution to the institution and his people during that time.

In 1909, following a particularly gruesome lynching in Springfield, Illinois, Du Bois was invited to join a group of liberal whites headed by William English Walling at a conference in New York City. There it was decided to form a permanent association to combat such atrocities. The New York conference urged Du Bois to merge the Niagara Movement with them to create the National Association for the Advancement of Colored People. The idea of such a merger was not unanimously welcomed. The fiery Boston editor, William Monroe Trotter, a Niagara Movement founder, refused to come into the new organization. He did not trust white leadership.

Mrs. Nina Du Bois and William E. B. Du Bois, circa 1910.

Du Bois, however, saw this association as broadening and strengthening the Negro's struggle. He agreed to be one of the five founding members and managed to persuade most of the membership of the Niagara Movement to go with him. He would not, however, accept the post of Association Secretary. The Secretary "raises money," he said, and "What I wanted to do was to write and to talk."

He was anxious to continue with his program of research started at Atlanta University, and although he knew that he would have to modify his program at the NAACP, he recalled, "After some difficulty, I persuaded them to let me found *The Crisis Magazine, A Record of the Darker Races.* With this monthly magazine I could discuss the Negro problem and tell white people and colored people just what the NAACP was and what it proposed to do. And so I changed from studying the Negro problem to propaganda."

The National Association for the Advancement of Colored People opened its offices in New York City at 20 Vesey Street. Here Du Bois was given office space for *The Crisis* and his small staff. He brought Nina and Yolande to New York where they moved into temporary housing in Brooklyn with a former Wilberforce student, Charles Burroughs. Later they moved into New York City where they took an apartment in the new Paul Laurence Dunbar Housing Cooperative. It was the beginning of a long association.

Part Four

THE National Association for the Advancement of Colored People opened its offices in New York City at 20 Vesey Street. Here Du Bois was given office space for *The Crisis* and a small staff. He brought his wife and daughter to New York from Atlanta where they moved into the home of Charles Burroughs, a former student at Wilberforce, who had a large residence in Flatbush. They remained with the Burroughs family until about 1920 when Du Bois secured an apartment in the new and fashionable Paul Laurence Dunbar Building.

James Weldon Johnson, writer, poet, diplomat and Du Bois' friend, joined the Association in 1916 as the Executive Secretary. He provided a helpful mediating influence between some of the members of the Executive Board and Du Bois. There was constant friction over the degree of autonomy that *The Crisis* should have. Du Bois was determined that it should be absolute. He did not consider the magazine a "house organ," but rather a journal of "opinion." As the editor-in-chief, it was his opinion that would get voice in the publication. So the years between 1915 and 1925 were filled with quarrels within the Association, some petty, some not, and the continued growth and development of both *The Crisis* and the Association.

Mary White Ovington

Joel E. Spingarn

Oswald Garrison Villard

William Stanley Braithwaite

Mary White Ovington, Joel Spingarn, Oswald Garrison Villard, William Stanley Braith-waite, J. Max Barber, and Du Bois were the editorial board of the NAACP's organ, *The Crisis*. Ovington, Villard and Spingarn were NAACP founders. Barber, former editor of *The Voice of the Negro*, in Atlanta, had been actively involved in the formation of the Niagara Movement. Braithwaite and Du Bois were lifelong friends.

W. E. B. Du Bois

J. Max Barber

THE CRISIS

A RECORD OF THE DARKER RACES

Volume One   NOVEMBER, 1910   Number One

Edited by W. E. BURGHARDT DU BOIS, with the co-operation of Oswald Garrison Villard, J. Max Barber, Charles Edward Russell, Kelly Miller, W. S. Braithwaite and M. D. Maclean.

CONTENTS

PUBLISHED MONTHLY BY THE

National Association for the Advancement of Colored People

AT TWENTY VESEY STREET   NEW YORK CITY

ONE DOLLAR A YEAR   TEN CENTS A COPY

Top, Marcus Garvey, the Jamaican nationalist whom Du Bois characterized as "imprac-
tical." Du Bois denied being anti-Garvey. Center, group of participants in program
celebrating the 50th Anniversary of the Emancipation Proclamation, 1913, New York
City. Bottom, *Birth of a Nation*, the anti-Negro motion picture that aroused the NAACP
and other groups against its showing.

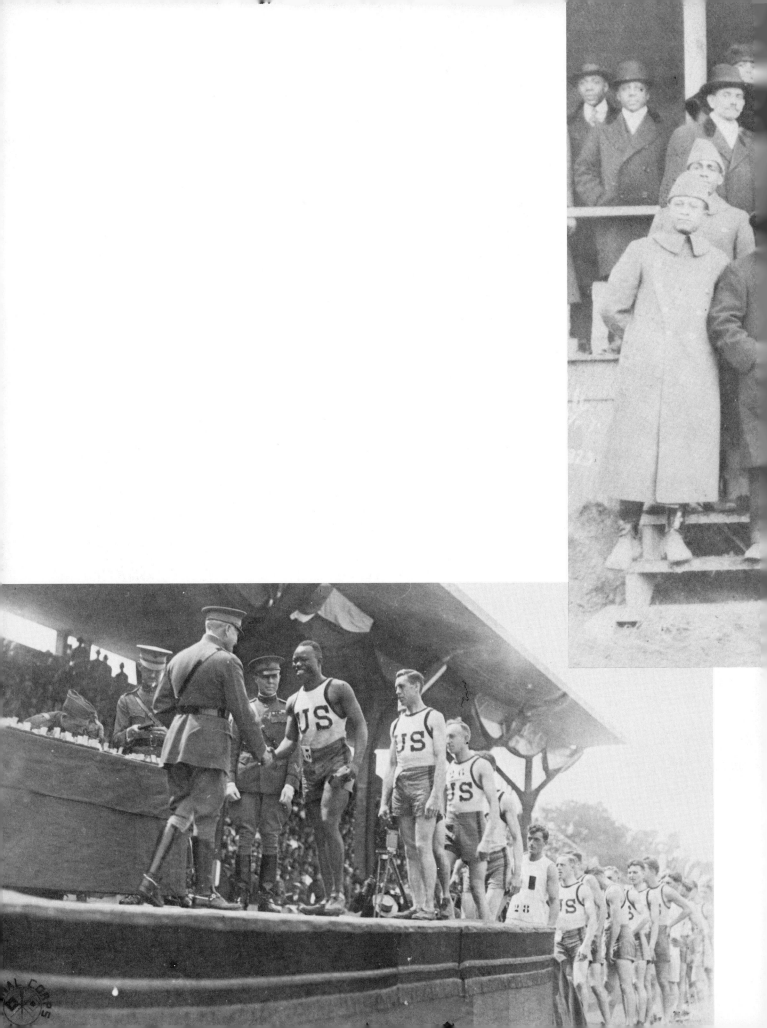

Above, World War I and Black soldiers leaving for France. Group at opening of Buffalo's Auditorium, Camp Upton, N.Y., 1917. Left, Sol Butler, U.S. representative in the Inter-Allied Games in Paris, receiving medal for winning in broad jump event with 24 feet, 9 and one-half inches, 1919.

Rioting broke out in cities across the United States in the years between 1915 and 1920. A particularly brutal riot took place in East St. Louis, Illinois, in 1917. The NAACP organized a parade to protest the terrorization of Black communities, and the Dyer anti-lynch bill was introduced in Congress in 1921. In front line of parade are Du Bois, James Weldon Johnson, Reverend Hutchins Bishop, and Jack Nail, prominent New York realtor.

50

Lynchings, race-riots, the mass migration of rural Blacks from the Southland to northern and midwestern cities, and finally, World War I, kept the pages of *The Crisis* filled with news and notices as well as the editorial opinions of Du Bois and others who wrote in to *The Crisis* with reports from across the country.

The NAACP authorized Du Bois to call for a "Pan-African Congress." In 1919, while in Paris, with the aid of Blaise Diagne, a Senegalese member of the French Parliament, Du Bois arranged for the First Pan-African Congress. It aroused tremendous interest. The 1919 meeting was held while the First World War combatants were meeting in Versailles to assure peace in Europe. The Paris Pan-African Congress passed resolutions and made demands for the indigenous peoples of Africa, which Du Bois then presented to the Peace Conference at Versailles. Fifty-seven delegates were present including sixteen Black Americans, twenty West Indians and twelve Africans. This Congress had been Du Bois' dream since the 1900 Paris Conference where he and Harold Williams, a West Indian lawyer had petitioned Queen Victoria for a Pan-African conference. Du Bois said, "We protested the treatment of the natives in the organization of South Africa, but we lost out on our hopes of a permanent organization."

The Third Pan-African Congress was held in Lisbon, Portugal, 1923. By this time Du Bois was thoroughly committed to developing the Pan-African Congress. The Lisbon session was particularly successful and significant. Efforts were made to hold the Congress somewhere on the continent of Africa. However, this was prevented by the controlling colonial powers. A Fourth Pan-African Congress was held in 1926 in New York City. Delegates from all sections of the United States attended, with large representation from the Caribbean and Latin America. But the Back-to-Africa movement launched by Marcus Garvey with its attendant publicity provided a fatal blow to Du Bois' Pan-African meetings for more than a decade.

Du Bois on lecture tour in Bowie, Oklahoma. It was on a similar tour when he visited Colorado Springs, that I first met W. E. B.

54

Many of the people who wrote in to *The Crisis* also invited Du Bois to come to their cities and towns to speak and to help in raising money for the local Branches of the National Association for the Advancement of Colored People. It was on one of these visits that I first met him.

It was 1920 and Dr. Du Bois included Colorado Springs, Colorado, on one of his speaking tours. My father, Reverend David A. Graham, an A.M.E. minister and organizer of a local chapter of the NAACP, invited Dr. Du Bois to spend his two nights in Colorado Springs at our house. Dr. Du Bois was speaking at my father's church, and so it was appropriate that he be my family's guest.

I recall that first supper with him and the questions that my father asked. Du Bois had returned shortly before from Paris where he had presented a plan for the decolonization of Africa to the Peace Conference at Versailles. My father wanted to know what its reception had been. I don't recall the answer, but I do remember that the conversation drifted around to Du Bois' experience as a student and young teacher in the South for the first time from his native Great Barrington, Massachusetts. He reminisced about the scarcity of teachers and how Black children could go to school only when they were not needed in the fields as farm hands. He told how in many areas Black teachers were not allowed by whites to come into the community, and how Black parents tried to protect the teachers who risked so much to teach their children.

After dinner he was taken to the "guest" room. I slept on the couch in my father's study. I was happy to have the great Dr. W. E. B. Du Bois sleeping upstairs in my little room.

In 1920 Du Bois was granted the Spingarn Medal, the highest honor the NAACP can bestow. His work in establishing the First Pan-African Congress was cited.

So *the Girl* marries

THE problem of marriage among American Negroes is a difficult one. On the one hand go conflicting philosophies: should we black folk breed children or commit biological suicide? On the other, should we seek larger sex freedom or closer conventional rules? Should we guide and mate our children like the French or leave the whole matter of sex intermingling to the chance of the street, like Americans? These are puzzling questions and all the more so because we do not often honestly face them.

I was a little startled when I became father of a girl. I scented far-off difficulties. But she became soon a round little bunch of Joy: plump and jolly, full of smiles and fun—a flash of twinkling legs and bubbling mischief. Always there on the broad campus of Atlanta University she was in scrapes and escapades—how many I never dreamed until years after: running away from her sleepy nurse; riding old Billy, the sage and dignified draft horse; climbing walls; bullying the Matron; cajoling the cooks and becoming the thoroughly spoiled and immeasurably loved Baby of the Campus. How far the spoiling had gone I became suddenly aware one summer, when we stopped a while to breathe the salt sea air at Atlantic City. This tot of four years marched beside me down the Boardwalk amid the unmoved and almost unnoticing crowd. She was puzzled. Never before in her memory had the world treated her quite so indifferently.

"Papa," she exclaimed at last, impatiently, "I guess they don't know I'm here!"

As the Girl grew so grew her problems: School; Multiplication Tables; Playmates; Latin; Clothes—Boys! No sooner had we faced one than the other loomed, the last lingered—the next threatened. She went to Kindergarten with her playmates of the Campus—kids and half-grown-ups. The half-grown-ups, Normal students, did me the special courtesy of letting the Girl dawdle and play and cut up. So when she came at the age of ten to the Ethical Culture School in New York there loomed the unlearned Multiplication Table; and a time we had! For despite all proposals of "letting the Child develop as it Will!", she must learn to read and count; and the school taught her—but at a price!

Then came the days of gawky growth; the impossible children of the street; someone to play with; wild tears at going to bed; excursions; games —and far, far in the offing, the shadow of the Fear of the Color Line.

I had a Grand Idea. Before the time loomed—before the Hurt pierced and lingered and festered, off to England she should go for high school and come back armed with manners and knowledge, cap-a-pie, to fight American race hate and insult. Off the Girl went to Bedale's, just as war thundered in the world. As a professor of Economics and History, I knew the war would be short—a few months. So away went Mother and Girl. Two mighty years rolled turbulently by and back came both through the Submarine Zone. The Girl had grown. She was a reticent stranger with whom soul revealing converse was difficult. I found myself groping for continual introductions.

Then came Latin. The English teacher talked Latin and his class at Bedale's romped with Caesar through a living Gallia. The American teacher in the Brooklyn Girl's High did not even talk English and regarded Latin as a crossword puzzle with three inches of daily solution. "Decline Stella!" "Conjugate Amo"; "What is the subject of 'Gallia est omnis divisa—' " "Nonsense," said the Girl (which was quite true), "I've dropped Latin!"

"But the colleges haven't," I moaned. "Why college?" countered the Girl.

Why indeed? I tried Cicero "pro Archia Poeta." The Girl was cold. Then I pleaded for my own spiritual integrity: "I have told 12 million to go to college—what will they say if you don't go?" The Girl admitted that that was reasonable but she said she was considering marriage and really thought she knew about all that schools could teach effectively. I, too, was reasonable and most considerate, despite the fact that I was internally aghast. This baby—married—My God!—but, of course, I said

Yolande Du Bois, in cap and gown, graduating from Fisk University, 1926. Yolande Du Bois' wedding to poet Countee Cullen in 1928 was a moving event for her father who wrote about her growing up and marriage in *The Crisis*. The wedding was at Salem Baptist Church, New York City, and the ceremony was performed by the groom's father, the Reverend Frederick A. Cullen, pastor of Salem Baptist Church.

aloud: Honorable state and all that; and "Go ahead, if you like—but how about a year in college as a sort of, well, introduction to life in general and for furnishing topics of conversation in the long years to come? How about it?" "Fair enough," said the Girl and she went to college.

Boys! queer animals. Hereditary enemies of Fathers-with-daughters and Mothers! Mother had chaperoned the Girl relentlessly through High School. Most Mothers didn't bother. It was a bore and one felt like the uninvited guest or the veritable Death's Head. The Girl didn't mind much, only—"Well, really Mother you don't need to go or even to sit up." But Mother stuck to her job. I've always had the feeling that the real trick was turned in those years, by a very soft-voiced and persistent Mother who was always hanging about unobtrusively. The boys liked her, the girls were good-naturedly condescending; the Girl laughed. It was so funny. Father, of course, was busy with larger matters and weightier problems, including himself.

Clothes. In the midst of high school came sudden clothes. The problem of raiment. The astonishing transformation of the hoyden and hiker and basket-ball expert into an amazing butterfly. We parents had expressed lofty distain for the new colored beauty parlors—straightening and bleaching, the very idea! But they didn't straighten, they cleaned and curled; they didn't whiten, they delicately darkened. They did for colored girls' style of beauty what two sophisticated centuries had been doing for blonde frights. When the finished product stood forth all silked and embroidered, briefly skirted and long-limbed with impudent lip-stick and jaunty toque—well, Thrift hung its diminished head and Philosophy stammered. What shall we do about our daughter's extravagant dress? The beauty of colored girls has increased 100% in a decade because they give to it time and trouble. Can we stop it? Should we? Where shall we draw the line, with good silk stockings at $1.95 per pair?

"Girl! You take so long to dress! I can dress in fifteen minutes."

"Yes—Mamma and you look it!" came the frankly unfilial answer.

College. College was absence and premonition. Empty absence and occasional letters and abrupt pauses. One wondered uneasily what they were doing with the Girl; *who* rather than what was educating her. Four years of vague uneasiness with flashes of hectic and puzzling vacations. Once with startling abruptness there arose the Shadow of Death—acute appendicitis; the hospital—the cold, sharp knife; the horror of waiting and the namelessly sweet thrill of recovery. Of course, all the spoiling began again and it literally rained silk and gold.

Absence, too, resulted in the unexpected increase in Parent-valuation. Mother was enshrined and worshipped by the absent Girl; no longer was she merely convenient and at times in the way. She was desperately adored. Even Father took on unaccustomed importance and dignity and found new place in the scheme of things. We both felt quite set up.

60

Then graduation and a Woman appeared in the family. A sudden woman—sedate, self-contained, casual, grown; with a personality—with wants, expenses, plans. "There will be a caller tonight."—"Tomorrow night I'm going out."

It was a bit disconcerting, this transforming of a rubber ball of childish joy into a lady whose address was at your own house. I acquired the habit of discussing the world with this stranger—as impersonally and coolly as possible: teaching—travel—reading—art—marriage. I achieved quite a detached air, letting the domineering daddy burst through only at intervals, when it seemed impossible not to remark—"It's midnight, my dear," and "when is the gentleman going? You need sleep!"

My part in Mate-selection was admittedly small but I flatter myself not altogether negligible. We talked the young men over—their fathers and grandfathers; their education; their ability to earn particular sorts of living; their dispositions. All this incidentally mind you—not didactically or systematically. Once or twice I went on long letter hunts for facts; usually facts were all too clear and only deductions necessary. What was the result? I really don't know. Sometimes I half suspect that the Girl arranged it all and that I was the large and solemn fly on the wheel. At other times I flatter myself that I was astute, secret, wise and powerful. Truth doubtless lurks between. So the Girl marries.

I remember the Boy came to me somewhat breathlessly one Christmas eve with a ring in his pocket. I told him as I had told others. "Ask her—she'll settle the matter; not I." But he was a nice boy. A rather unusual boy with the promise of fine manhood. I wished him luck. But I did not dare plead his cause. I had learned—well, I had learned.

Thus the world grew and blossomed and changed and so the Girl marries. It is the end of an era—a sudden break and beginning. I rub my eyes and readjust my soul. I plan frantically. It will be a simple, quiet ceremony—

"In a church, father!"

"Oh! in a church? Of course, in a church. Well, a church wedding would be a little larger, but—"

"With Countée's father and the Reverend Frazier Miller assisting."

"To be sure—well, that is possible and, indeed, probable."

"And there will be sixteen bridesmaids."

One has to be firm somewhere—"But my dear! who ever *heard* of sixteen bridesmaids!"

"But Papa, there are eleven Moles, and five indispensables and Margaret—"

Why argue? What has to be, must be; and this evidently had to be. I struggled faintly but succumbed. Now with sixteen bridesmaids and ten ushers must go at least as many invited guests.

You who in travail of soul have struggled with the devastating puzzle of selecting a small bridge party out of your total of twenty-five intimate friends, lend me your sympathy! For we faced the world-shattering problem of selecting for two only children, the friends of a pastor with twenty-five years service in one church; and the friends of a man who knows good people in forty-five states and three continents. I may recover from it but I shall never look quite the same. I shall always have a furtive feeling in my soul. I know that at the next corner I shall meet my Best Friend and remember that I forgot to invite him. Never in all eternity can I explain.

The Bride and Her Attendants.

The Misses Roberta Bosley, Ruth McGhee, Anna Welmon, Harriet Pickens, Etta Burwell, Helen Reynolds, Thelma Garland, Hilda Anderson, Alice Mundy, Gladys Byram, Ruth DeMond, Chita McCard, Kathyrn McCracken, Mae Wright and Constance Murphy; together with Miss Margaret Welmon, Maid of Honor; and the Misses Annie Brown and Margaret Pennypacker, Soloists.

The Groom and His Ushers.

The Messrs. Harold Jackman, Edward Perry, Langston Hughes, Embrey Bonner, Arna Bontemps, William Brown, Robert Weaver, William Alphaeus Hunton, 2nd, Albert Walker, Alex F. Miller and William Howell; together with Melville Charlton, Organist, the Reverend George Frazier Miller, and the parents of the bride and groom.

Countee Cullen, groom and poet.

63

How can I say: "Bill, I just forgot you!" Or "My *dear* Mrs. Blubenski, I didn't remember where on earth you were or indeed if you were at all or ever!" No, one can't say such things. I shall only stare at them pleadingly, in doubt and pain, and slink wordlessly away.

Thirteen hundred were bidden to the marriage and no human being has one thousand three hundred friends! Five hundred came down to greet the bride at a jolly reception which I had originally planned for twenty-five. Of course, I was glad they were there. I expanded and wished for a thousand. Three thousand saw the marriage and a thousand waited on the streets. It was a great pageant; a heart-swelling throng; birds sang and Melville Charlton let the organ roll and swell beneath his quivering hands. A sweet young voice sang of Love; and then came the holy:

"Freudig gefuert, Ziehet dahin!"

The symbolism of that procession was tremendous. It was not the mere marriage of a maiden. It was not simply the wedding of a fine young poet. It was the symbolic march of young and black America. America, because there was Harvard, Columbia, Smith, Brown, Howard, Chicago, Syracuse, Penn and Cornell. There were three Masters of Arts and fourteen Bachelors. There were poets and teachers, actors, artists and students. But it was not simply conventional America—it had a dark and shimmering beauty all its own; a calm and high restraint and sense of new power; it was a new race; a new thought; a new thing rejoicing in a ceremony as old as the world. (And after it all and before it, such a jolly, happy crowd; some of the girls even smoked cigarettes!)

Why should there have been so much of pomp and ceremony—flowers and carriages and silk hats; wedding cake and wedding music? After all marriage in its essence is and should be very simple: a clasp of friendly hands; a walking away together of Two who say: "Let us try to be One and face and fight a lonely world together!" What more? Is that not enough? Quite; and were I merely white I should have sought to make it end with this.

But it seems to me that I owe something extra to an Idea, a Tradition. We who are black and panting up hurried hills of hate and hindrance— we have got to establish new footholds on the slipping by-paths through which we come. They must at once be footholds of the free and the eternal, the new and the enthralled. With all of our just flouting of white convention and black religion, some things remain eternally so—Birth, Death, Pain, Mating, Children, Age. Ever and anon we must point to these truths and if the pointing be beautiful with music and ceremony or bare with silence and darkness—what matter? The width or narrowness of the gesture is a matter of choice. That one will have it stripped to the essence. It is still good and true. This soul wants color with bursting cords and scores of smiling eyes in happy raiment. It must be as this soul wills. The Girl wills this. So the Girl marries.

W. E. B. D.

Du Bois was not against relaxation, and when he could, he got away with friends as in these photos, circa 1920.

Du Bois in first car.

Du Bois, Mrs. Nina Du Bois, and James Weldon Johnson in New York City.

66

John Hope, president, Atlanta University and life-long Du Bois friend. Hope's untimely death altered Du Bois' plans for extensive research project and publications program.

Part Five

Du BOIS traveled all over the United States and in 1926 made his first trip to Russia. He said: "I became interested in Russia and had tried to follow the events of the Revolution of 1917, but there wasn't very good news coverage in the United States. . . . In 1926 I made my first trip to Russia. I traveled rather widely to Leningrad, to Moscow, Gorky . . . to the Ukraine. My interest in Russia became very great and my belief in her work and her future tremendous.

"On the other hand in the U.S. after the World War and after the beginning of rather feverish prosperity, I began to realize that something was going wrong with our economic organization. The income of *The Crisis* began to fall off and I began to see that Negroes were losing their jobs, the opposition to them in the trade union ranks was still strong, and it was clear that *The Crisis*, as the depression went on, was not going to pay for itself—it was not going to be self-supporting. Now that brought an inevitable change. So long as *The Crisis* was self-supporting, I could be practically independent within certain wide limits in what I was saying to the public. But if the National Association had to support *The Crisis*, then of course the National Association had a right to have the last word as to what was to be said and it would become an organ. Organs are never read because they are not interesting. They have to say whatever the Board of Trustees vote. I made up my mind that my job in propaganda was over.

"My independence on *The Crisis* had to be given up and it was time for me to return to my ivory tower and go to work in study and writing. So in 1933, I resigned from the NAACP. . . ."

In retrospect W. E. B. glossed over a very unpleasant time. James Weldon Johnson had resigned to go to Fisk to teach, and Walter White had taken his place. The rivalry was intense. "At the invitation of my good friend John Hope I went down to Atlanta University and stayed there ten years. Unfortunately Hope died, the year after I'd gone there. Worked himself to death."

Hope's sudden death in 1936 was a shock to Du Bois. He realized that without the firm backing which Dr. Hope, as president of Atlanta University had given him, his undertaking would be much harder.

In February 1938, his seventieth birthday was celebrated in Atlanta with a banquet attended by friends from all over the country. The bronze bust of him by Alexander Portnoff was presented to the university, and poet William Stanley Braithwaite read lines he had written for the occasion. Dr. Rufus Clement had succeeded Hope as president of A.U.

For sheer physical energy, few men thirty years younger could have challenged Du Bois' output during those ten years at Atlanta. He went into every part of the South, talking with Black peasant workers and small landowners, with every land-grant college head and with leading educators North and South. He organized and presided over conferences, addressed meetings, prepared and published each year the *Atlanta University Studies*, edited a quarterly magazine, *Phylon*, carried a teaching load, and supervised a large group of assistants. In addition he wrote and published his monumental work, *Black Reconstruction*, followed by *Black Folk, Then and Now* (1939) and *Dusk of Dawn* (1940). He was editor-in-chief for a project of the Phelps-Stokes Fund to prepare an *Encyclopedia of the Negro*. He also made a trip around the world one summer vacation.

Du Bois with leading Japanese professors in Tokyo to discuss common problems of colored people throughout the world, 1936.

Nonetheless at the August, 1944, meeting of the Board of Trustees at Atlanta University, President Rufus Clement "reluctantly" proposed to the Board of Trustees that they would have to let Dr. Du Bois go. Again, it was felt that the social reforms being implemented in the University's Sociology Department were threatening the school's financial support. The Board voted to retire Du Bois as professor and head of the Department of Sociology at Atlanta University. He was shocked.

His old friend and long-time supporter, Arthur Spingarn, refused to see it as a catastrophe. With the support of Dr. Louis Wright, Chairman of the board of the NAACP, Du Bois was invited to return to the NAACP as director of Research. He would no longer be editing *The Crisis*, but would be "free to write and speak as he wished and to devote himself to special foreign aspects of the race problem." This had reference to renewing the work of the Pan-African Congresses. The board endorsed this idea since he was not to be involved in the regular organization, and the African thrust to racial advancement was entirely outside the planned scope of NAACP activity, therefore open to Du Bois.

It was necessary for Dr. Du Bois to relocate his residence to New York City. When Du Bois returned to Atlanta he had built a home for Mrs. Du Bois in Baltimore, near the Morgan College campus. Nina Du Bois had no wish to return to Atlanta, which she never ceased to view as the culprit in her infant son's death. Now she was not interested in uprooting again.

I was now on the staff of the NAACP so I made finding an apartment for my idol my special project. I was fortunate. I had set my mind on 409 Edgecombe, a building, physically and psychologically, at the *top* of Harlem. Only recently had important Blacks moved in: municipal judges, physicians, city officials; and the building presented a clean polished elegance. Now we secured a small top floor apartment for Dr. Du Bois. Through the windows of the sitting room and bedroom was a magnificent view of the Hudson River, the Palisades, the entire span of the George Washington Bridge and far below, blocks of city streets. For the next six years, this was Du Bois' home away from his Baltimore residence.

Photograph of the Board of Directors of *The Encyclopedia of the Negro:* Left to right—Miss Otelia Cromwell, Monroe N. Work, Charles H. Wesley, Benjamin Brawley, W. E. B. Du Bois, Eugene Kinckle Jones, Alain Locke, Waldo G. Leland. (Center) James Weldon Johnson, Charles T. Loram. (Rear) W. D. Weatherford, A. A. Schomburg, Joel E. Spingarn, Clarence S. Marsh, Anson Phelps Stokes, W. A. Avery, James H. Dillard, Miss Florence Read, Mordecai W. Johnson. Photo taken in Washington, D.C., May 16, 1936.

Du Bois, the elder statesman, head of the Sociology Department at Atlanta University, receives an honorary degree and ceremonial plaudits on occasion of his seventieth birthday. Below, Du Bois speaking during 70th Birthday banquet at Atlanta University, 1938.

70th Birthday celebrated at Atlanta University. At the banquet table are standing, left to right—Charles S. Johnson, Yolande Du Bois (now divorced from Countee Cullen), James Weldon Johnson, Ira De A. Reid, Rufus Clement (the successor to John Hope as president of Atlanta University), William Stanley Braithwaite, Du Bois, Mrs. Du Bois, and Joel Spingarn. The woman next to Du Bois is unidentified.

Top left, Du Bois with Sterling Brown, poet and professor of literature at Howard University, and Dorothy Maynor, the concert artist. Top right, Du Bois and Dr. Nnamdi Azikiwe, then leader of the National Council of Nigeria and the Cameroons. Dr. Azikiwe later became Governor-General of independent Nigeria. Picture taken about 1930. Below, Du Bois and group in Springfield, Illinois, in front of Lincoln's tomb, 1941. He laid wreath on tomb.

Above, Du Bois confers with Dr. Mary Mc-
Leod Bethune and Dr. Horace Mann Bond.
Lower right, with Metz T. P. Locard, the Sor-
bonne educated editor of the Chicago *De-
fender* newspaper.

Above, Du Bois and Governor
William Hastie of the Virgin
Islands at NAACP Conference
in Connecticut, 1947. Left,
Du Bois relaxes at the Cam-
bridge Rod and Gun Club in
Maine, a favorite resort.

Part Six

THE return to the NAACP fold was a mixed blessing. It placed him back in New York at the nexus of activity, and in the environment of like-minded people. But Walter White, now the Executive Secretary, was difficult. The two men clashed frequently. Du Bois said: "Immediately (upon coming back) I ran into trouble. We had agreed there were certain things, particularly connected with Africa and its development, which I would like to take up. I wanted two offices, one for myself and one for my secretary and library. That was all agreed to and I came back. I didn't get an office at all. They didn't seem to be able to find one, or Walter didn't. I couldn't get a clear program and I began to realize that what Walter White had in mind was that I should write speeches and reports and represent him. Which was not what I had in mind, at all.

"I finally did get a Pan-African Congress, or rather the trade unionists in Africa got one and invited me to Manchester, England in 1945. There I met some of the great . . . leaders of Africa—Nkrumah of Ghana, Johnson of Liberia, and Kenyatta of Kenya. I began to see the new spirit that was starting in Africa. I had been a consultant at the UN for the NAACP when it was formed in 1945. When I came back it was proposed that we appeal to the United Nations and ask them to take up the matter of the treatment of Negroes in the United States. I edited a report and got other well-equipped people to write different chapters. Walter made difficulty about that. He wanted to write a preface, which wasn't needed because my work in that was the preface.

"Some inkling of our difficulties got out to the press. I didn't send it to the press, but I told the Board of Directors afterwards, that if the press had asked me I would have told them because there wasn't anything secret about it. I was pre-emptorily dismissed in '48 after I had been there 4 years."

Sometime after returning to the NAACP, Du Bois had, without consulting White, accepted a place on the board of directors of the Council on African Affairs, a small organization which was disseminating information among Americans on the state of African colonies, exposing their exploitation and endeavoring to establish closer relations between Africans and Afro-Americans. Chairman of the Council was Dr. Max Yergan, whom Du Bois knew only slightly, but he knew Dr. Alphaeus Hunton, one of its executives, well. Hunton was a former professor at Howard University, whose family in Virginia were old friends of Du Bois. Paul Robeson was also a member of the Board. It was the Council on African Affairs which made it possible for Dean Dixon, a Juilliard School of Music honor graduate, to conduct a symphony orchestra in New York's Town Hall.

About the time that Du Bois was leaving the NAACP, Dr. Yergan lost his position with the Council. As Du Bois was free, he was urged to become chairman of the organization. He hesitated to accept this executive responsibility, but with the promised assistance of Paul (Robeson) and Alphaeus (Hunton), both of whom he regarded somewhat in the light of gifted sons, he considered the move. When he was also offered the top floor offices of Frederick Field, a backer of the Council, for his office, he accepted. The offices of the Council at 23 West 26th Street were ample. Du Bois moved in and the library was properly set up, the pictures and drapes hung, an African coat of armor from the Sudan and several pieces of Benin sculpture arranged, and he was "at home" in his new quarters at the Council on African Affairs.

Du Bois' identification card as representative of NAACP at Founding Convention of the United Nations, San Francisco, 1945.

Du Bois standing in front of portrait of Frederick Douglass in his apartment, 409 Edgecombe, New York City, 1946.

Du Bois and Walter White in an unusual photograph, with William Stanley Braithwaite. The tension that existed between White and Du Bois caused Du Bois to be "retired" for the second time, only four years after he returned from his Atlanta "retirement." He turned then to working for Peace as a method of solving the problems of Race in a worldwide setting. Du Bois, Braithwaite and White were all tenants at 409 Edgecombe.

79

Part Seven

THE winter of 1948–49 brought personal heartbreak to Du Bois. His wife had a stroke. He had her brought to a New York hospital for treatment, but she was soon longing for her home in Morgan Park, Baltimore. Their daughter, Yolande, taught in the Baltimore high school system. She was lonely. Du Bois accompanied her to Baltimore as soon as she was able to be moved.

Also, he did not go to the American Continental Congress for World Peace, nor to any other meetings to which he was invited. He had little to do with the setting up or plans of the Peace Information Center. This was a modest undertaking on the part of American delegates to the Paris Peace Congress. The Information Center sought to bring information to the people concerning world-wide efforts to prevent further wars. He did consent to be Chairman of the Center with an Executive Secretary who attended to the day by day details. We all helped in getting out a "Peace-gram."

Mrs. Nina Du Bois, circa 1940.

Du Bois meets Paul Robeson in Paris during World Peace Conference, April, 1949. It was the beginning of a time of trial for the two men. Paul Robeson had been making the historic "off-the-cuff" remarks at the Salle Pleyel, at the same time I was landing in Paris at Orly airport. Those remarks created the storm around him, that never really died. Paul had appeared unexpectedly at the Paris Peace Congress and was rushed to the platform where he was urged to say "a few words" to the cheering delegates. It seems that he said he did not believe black workers dragged into an imperialist war would fight white workers . . . even if they were Russians. That set off the shock waves felt around the world. But I was unaware of this when the orchestra in the Paris' Hotel Claridge struck up "Old Man River" at the sight of his huge figure making its way across the dining room to the Du Bois table. He and Du Bois greeted each other warmly as the old and dear friends they were. After a brief conversation, Paul was off almost immediately for Norway and the continuation of his concert tour. We wished him "Bon Voyage."

Mrs. Du Bois' death early that spring devastated her husband. After her burial in the family plot at Great Barrington where she was placed beside her beloved little boy, Du Bois returned to his Harlem apartment. For a time he was inconsolable, and withdrew from all activities. He flagellated himself in an agony of remorse. He blamed himself and said, "Poor Nina, I should have stayed with her—I should never have left her so much. I should have made her understand what I was trying to do. She never understood—she never understood!"

It was not until the spring when he received an invitation to speak at an International Youth Festival in Europe that he began to show any interest. Also his granddaughter, Du Bois Williams, now a sturdy sixteen-year-old, wanted to attend this festival. So in June they flew off to Prague, Czechoslovakia. Du Bois lingered in Europe and was in Paris when he received a transatlantic telephone call and a cable. The first informed him that the New York Labor Party had decided to run him as the Labor candidate for the U.S. Senate. The idea seemed utterly ludicrous to him! But the arguments presented were impressive and he promised to "think it over." Then came the cable from Abbott Simon, executive secretary of the Peace Information Center, informing him that the Department of Justice had demanded that the Center register as "agents of a foreign principal." Before leaving Paris he cabled one word to the New York Labor Party: "Accept."

Du Bois agreed to run for the U.S. Senate on the Labor Party ticket, August, 1950. That campaign was an amazing feat. He was then eighty-two years old, but George Murphy, the outspoken maverick of the Baltimore newspaper clan, his astute campaign manager, tells that "his zeal and sheer physical endurance wore me out!" He made speeches from one end of the state to the other, traveling short distances by automobile, otherwise by plane. He made seven broadcasts and held many press conferences. His last speech in the city of New York was at a gathering of 17,000 persons at Madison Square Garden on October 24. Later he wrote:

"On the whole I enjoyed this unique excursion into political activity. I encountered little open race prejudice, though of course few New Yorkers wanted to be represented in Washington by a Negro—because of their prejudice and also because they suspected I was more Negro than American. To counteract this, I made no special appeal to the Negro vote as such. I wanted the people of New York to know that as Senator I would represent the interests of the state and not merely those of one minority group. At the same time, I knew and Negroes knew, that I would regard Negro emancipation as the prime prerequisite to American freedom. The Negro voter in Harlem knew that no candidate would defend Negro rights as I would; he also knew that I could not possibly be elected!"

Du Bois was astonished by a vote of 205,729. He said, "It was a fine adventure."

Part Eight

CHRISTMAS, 1950, my mother and my surviving son, David, spent the Christmas holidays with me at my small house in St. Albans. We had a festive Christmas dinner in my brother's home in New York. All of my brothers were then engaged in working in the New York area. Du Bois was spending Christmas with his daughter in Baltimore. During Christmas week I had a telephone call from Du Bois and after inquiring about the family and our holiday, he asked, "Would you like to spend New Year's Eve with me?" His voice did not have its usual timbre, and I said simply, "I'd love to!"

And so, as the year 1951 came in, our future was settled. Du Bois maintained that he was "selfish" and "too old," but I knew that I had been in love with him for a long time. He had dominated my life to the extent that no other man could come near me. But my love made no demands. The fact that we shared work together was enough. Now, that was no longer true, for either of us. We set the date for a quiet wedding at my house.

Before we could carry out our plan the news came that he, Abbott Simon, Kyrle Elkin, the treasurer, Sylvia Soloff, office secretary and Elizabeth Moos, the former executive secretary of the Peace Information Center, had been indicted for "not having registered as agents of a foreign principal." The burden of proving that they were not such agents was on the defense. They faced, if convicted, a five-year prison sentence plus a fine of $10,000.

"How," Du Bois asked, "does a man go about proving he is not a thief?"

News of the indictment electrified Harlem. Whether or not they agreed with all "the Old Man's" policies, every Negro in the country knew that W. E. B. Du Bois wasn't anyone's "agent." The plans for marriage on February 27 were scrapped and in a short, private ceremony, with only my son David and a lawyer friend as witnesses, W. E. B. and I were married on February 14, 1951. After the short ceremony, David and I returned to St. Albans and Du Bois was driven back to his apartment at 409 Edgecombe Avenue. We decided to continue with our original plans for the wedding ceremony at my house. Du Bois said I wanted to be sure that the "shot-gun" ceremony was official.

Yolande came up in time for Du Bois' eighty-third birthday dinner at Small's Paradise, a Harlem nightclub that had been volunteered following the cancellation of the dinner by the Essex House. The dinner was sponsored by The Council on African Affairs and the backers of the now-closed Peace Information Center. The well-known sociologist Dr. E. Franklin Frazier of Howard University was chairman of the dinner committee. Some three hundred people made reservations for the celebration which was now a major fund-raising effort.

The night of the dinner was memorable. The place was packed to the point of suffocation. Many people could not get to their seats and the crowd spilled out into the streets. Belford Lawson, the national head of the Alpha Phi Alpha fraternity, made a fighting speech, Paul Robeson sang and spoke, Frazier presided and spoke. There were many cakes holding the eighty-three candles and we cut them right there so that all could share in their delicious richness.

Du Bois had caught a bad cold while speaking at an American Labor Party rally on an evening that was mixed blizzard of rain and snow. By the day following his birthday party, he was so hoarse that his physician feared he was on the edge of pneumonia and ordered him to bed. Prospects for our wedding on Tuesday looked grim. The doctor promised to have him on his feet for the ceremony, with the promise that immediately after, we would leave for Nassau, where Du Bois could get rest and sunshine.

Returning to New York, we soon set out on a campaign to win support against Du Bois' indictment. A "National Committee to Defend Dr. W. E. B. Du Bois and Associates in the Peace Information Center" had been formed, and the trial had been put off until November. Our first stop was in Chicago, then to Gary, Indiana, St. Paul, Minnesota, Portland, Oregon, Seattle, Washington, and down to San Francisco and sunny Los Angeles. Attendance at the mass meetings in Oakland and San Francisco totaled well over two thousand. Du Bois with three defendants of the Peace Information Center indicted with him: Kyrle Elkin, Sylvia Soloff, and Abbott Simon (one defendant, Mrs. Elizabeth Moos, was hurrying back from Europe to stand trial with her co-workers). I am with the group just before going into courthouse in Washington for the arraignment, February, 1951.

The time for the ceremony arrived and the minister was late. David brought me this message from W. E. B., who was quite calm and unruffled. The message: "Tell your mother we do not have to be married twice. Tonight we leave on our honeymoon, whether Reverend McGowan gets here or not."

The minister did arrive and so, preceded by Yolande as my matron of honor, accompanied by my son, surrounded by family and friends and with music in the air, for the second time we promised to "love and cherish." After the cake-cutting, the change to traveling suits, we were off to the airport and Nassau for our honeymoon. We would worry about the impending trial later. It had been scheduled for November.

Meanwhile, I set about finding a house that was right for Du Bois and me, and we learned that Arthur Miller, the playwright, wanted to sell his two-family building in Brooklyn Heights, N.Y. When I first saw 31 Grace Court, it was love at first sight. The garden, with cherry and peach trees, and a magnolia, was enough for me . . . , but combined with the house with frescoed drawing room and fireplace, made it perfect. We moved into our first home during the summer of 1951, before the trial.

Du Bois and I are married at my home in St. Albans, Long Island, February 27, 1951.

The trial opened on November 8, 1951. For two weeks we sat in the crowded, stuffy courtroom, Lillian Elkin and I, separated from our husbands, who were on the other side of the railing on the criminals' bench. We were frankly terrified at what might happen. As the days dragged by the entire affair took on an air of unreality. From the beginning Judge Matthew F. McGuire impressed me as being intelligent and even kindly. His opening remarks were significant:

> The point in this case is whether or not this organization acted as an agent or in a capacity similar to that for a foreign organization or foreign political power, whether advocating peace, advocating this, or advocating that. They can advocate the distribution of wealth; they can advocate that all redheaded men be shot. It doesn't make any difference what they advocate.

The prosecution rested its case during the morning of November 20, and the defense began its argument for a judgment of acquittal. Following lunch, Vito Marcantonio was to present witnesses for the defense. He told the judge that only one witness was to be presented, Dr. Du Bois. "He is ready." Marcantonio said, and he added casually to the judge, "Dr. Albert Einstein has offered to appear as a character witness for Dr. Du Bois." Judge McGuire fixed Marcantonio with a long look, and then adjourned court for lunch.

When court resumed, Judge McGuire took up the motions of the morning, the second one, to move for acquittal. Judge McGuire spoke:

> The Government has alleged that the Peace Information Center was the agent of a foreign principal. They proved the existence of the Peace Information Center. They certainly proved the existence of the World Council of Peace. . . . But applying the test, as laid down here, in a case which, presumably is the law of the land . . . in this case, the Government has failed to support, on the evidence adduced, the allegations laid down in the indictment. . . . So, therefore, the motion, under the circumstances, for a judgement of acquittal will be granted.

We were free. That next afternoon we went home to 31 Grace Court.

On the morning of February 14, 1952, our first wedding anniversary, we were notified by the U.S. State Department that our application for passports to attend a conference in Rio de Janeiro, were being held, because, "it appears that your proposed travel would be contrary to the best interests of the United States."

Defendants Reunion, November, 1956, with their families.

Desk with bound first editions of Du Bois' books in living room of home at 31 Grace Court, Brooklyn Heights, 1959. Binding done as a gift from the New York Furriers Union.

Great Barrington, Massachusetts, where Du Bois was born is in the Western part of the state. He took me there for my first visit after our marriage. He has written, "I was born by a golden river and in the shadow of two great hills." Great Barrington, nestled in the valley of the Housatonic river is in the heart of the majestic Berkshire mountains. We found remnants of the fireplace that had once belonged to the Burghardt family, and I thought of the men and the women that were my husband's forebears. Amidst a tumbledown ruin, which had been Du Bois grandfather's house, a large stone fireplace stood with part of the chimney still intact. Here in Great Barrington, Du Bois reminisced about his free and happy childhood.

In May, 1953, we traveled to Long Cay, a small, almost deserted island at the southern tip of the Bahamas. Here, we knew W. E. B.'s paternal grandfather had been born. We searched in vain for exact records of Dr. James Du Bois' family. We did find one aristocratic looking old lady who was said to be his descendant. This "sentimental journey" is described in *His Day Is Marching On*. Passports were not required for the Bahamas journey, only proof of citizenship.

Father Thomas, parish priest on Long Cay, in the Bahamas, helped us to search for other Du Bois family members on the island. An old woman we met told Du Bois, "You *are* a Du Bois. You have the eyes and nose and you have the stance." Her mother was a Du Bois, and she relayed the information that most people on the island were related, "more or less." Here we are on the beautiful beach, in an 18th century graveyard, Father Thomas, our host and guide, standing in the doorway of his church.

By the spring of 1952 Du Bois was campaigning for the Progressive Party. Here being welcomed by committee at Los Angeles' Union Station.

Du Bois on his 87th birthday, February 23, 1955. I am being helpful.

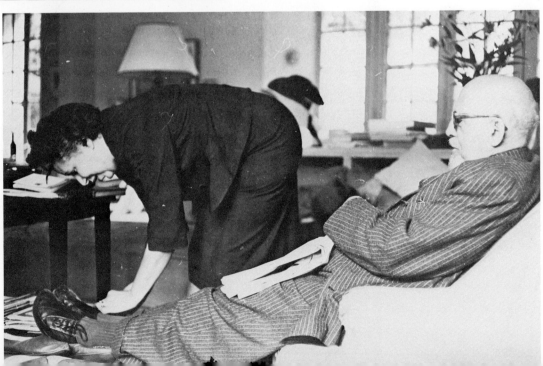

Du Bois working on a non-salaried basis for The Council on African Affairs spoke frequently on African and Afro-American history. Paul Robeson and W. Alphaeus Hunton worked with Du Bois in the Council until the arbitrary closing of the N.Y. office in November, 1956. Du Bois worked at home after the Council closed. He completed the Mansart Trilogy during this time.

The unveiling of the bronze bust of Du Bois by sculptor William Zorach took place at the Schomburg Research Center of the New York Public Library. Curator Jean Blackwell accepted the head for the famed archive.

Part Nine

NINETEEN fifty-eight was the year the people of the United States celebrated the 90th birthday of W. E. B. Du Bois. In New England, the *Berkshire Eagle* told of his beginnings and hailed him as the "most distinguished son" of that county. The *Pittsburgh Courier, Afro-American*, and New York's *National Guardian* brought out special supplements with pictures illustrating high points in his life; two Negro colleges invited him to come and accept honorary degrees. Immediately after the big reception held at the Roosevelt Hotel in New York City, similar affairs were held in Detroit, Chicago, San Francisco, Los Angeles, Nashville, Baltimore, and Washington. On February 7 he had received the following letter from Editorial Offices of *Who's Who in America*:

> "This year marks the publication of Volume 30, the Sixtieth Anniversary Edition of *Who's Who in America*. . . .We are paying special honor to the twenty-eight biographees of Volume I who have been continuously listed in all thirty editions. . . . You are one of that honored group. It gives me great pleasure to invite you to our Sixtieth Anniversary celebration, held at the Arts Club of Chicago on March 1."

Of the five biographees who attended this celebration, Du Bois was the eldest having begun his ninety-first year just five days before.

Nineteen fifty-eight was the year in which the people of the United States celebrated the ninetieth birthday of W. E. B. Du Bois. There were celebrations all over the country: New York, Detroit, San Francisco, Los Angeles, Nashville, Baltimore and Chicago. These photographs taken at the Chicago observation include Sidney Williams, noted Africanist and former Urban League executive. Margaret Goss Burroughs, artist Bernard Goss with his birthday portrait of W. E. B., and other well wishers.

Du Bois speaking to an assembly of prominent Chicagoans. Among those sharing the platform are Margaret Burroughs, curator of the Du Sable Museum of Afro-American History, editor, Metz Lochard, Truman Gibson, Sr. and Judge Sidney A. Jones.

During Du Bois days as a student at Fisk University, there was no Phi Beta Kappa chapter on the campus. When he returned for an honorary degree in his ninetieth year, he was inducted into the Fisk chapter and presented his Phi Beta Kappa key.

Du Bois receiving honorary degree from Fisk University; citation read by Dr. Stephen Wright, President of Fisk, March, 1958.

107

Sailing for Europe on the *Liberte*.

We had been deprived of passports since 1952. In June, 1958, the Supreme Court handed down a decision which wiped out a political affadavit as a prerequisite for obtaining a passport. Paul Robeson and many other Americans were now free to travel. Soon Du Bois was receiving fresh invitations from various countries, and we decided on a long, leisurely trip—crossing by steamer rather than on an overnight plane. August 8 we sailed on the S.S. *Liberte* for Southampton, England. Yolande came up from Baltimore, friends brought flowers and chilled champagne on board and David dashed around snapping pictures.

David Graham Du Bois

108

Above, Yolande Du Bois Williams with a friend sees us off for Europe on an unforgettable voyage.

Robeson's residence in Maida Vale, London.

Arriving in London, we learned that the Robesons, who were on a concert tour on the continent, were turning over their flat to us for the duration of our stay. During our three-week stay, W. E. B. made only one speech; that was to a large assemblage of African students. One evening a group of African students in native dress assembled in the garden "to honor the Father of Pan-Africanism." They put on a performance of music and dancing. For two hours African drums throbbed through the London night. Our friends combined with friends of the Robesons to see that we were well entertained. While in London an invitation came from Paul Breman, a Dutch scholar of some repute, for Dr. Du Bois to speak at The Hague and to have a television interview. He was offered expenses for himself and his wife and an honorarium for the lecture. Du Bois accepted the invitation.

We went to Holland across the channel by boat. The crossing was smooth and just long enough to be enjoyable. Paul, a slight, tousle-haired young man, met us at the landing and drove us from Amsterdam to The Hague. A reasonably large audience of middle-aged scholars had gathered to hear Du Bois' remarks. Afterward we spent the night as guests of Paul's in-laws in a nearby village.

I will always think of Paul Breman as a forerunner of the youth of the world who in the sixties and seventies are seeing to it that the world does change.

The meeting at The Hague, September 10, 1958.

We took a scenic train from Amsterdam to Paris where our good friend Elizabeth Moos met us. Paris was gripped in the tension of the Algerian War, and every dark-skinned person seemed suspect. There were even armed guards standing at the gate to the Luxembourg Gardens, but Du Bois with his typically haughty air, gave them hard stares and we walked past and into the lovely gardens. It is difficult to say which month is best to spend in the Luxembourg Gardens. This September the trees were beginning to cloak themselves in fall colors and all the flowers seemed to glow from within. The air seemed filled with a golden mist and the children's tiny boats sailed across the pond in the gentlest of breezes.

Upon being told by a member of the Peace Council that the Algerian War was tearing France apart (political organizations and families) and that since being forced out of Vietnam, so-called "patriotic" Frenchmen were determined to hold on to Algeria under the assumption that it was simply an extension of France, Du Bois responded, "And, of course, the Algerians do not agree. Algeria is Africa—and like all Africa must be free from outside domination."

We visited Paul and Hazel Strand, good friends, who lived in a tiny village on the Seine, seventy-five or eighty kilometers from Paris. Paul and Hazel lived in a remodeled farmhouse—big beam-ceiling rooms, with enough modern appliances for convenience without spoiling its old fashioned peasant charm. Paul was an artist-photographer and after a wonderful supper we looked at his fine original pictures projected on the screen, and then drove back to Paris in Elizabeth Moos's rented automobile.

It was late in the evening when we reached Paris, but even though it was a Sunday evening we still felt it strange that every shop was closed and shuttered. No groups sitting at tables on the sidewalks and no couples strolling about . . . a smothering blanket seemed to lay over all.

The next morning I was down early looking for newspapers. The stand where we usually got them had none, and the usually cheerful newsman was surly and noncommittal. Later, when I returned with a couple of papers I told my husband of the response I had been given by the ordinarily friendly tradespeople. Then we read of the victory of DeGaulle's party in the elections. Du Bois commented, "Celebrations by the people would certainly seem to be lacking."

A few days later we flew from Paris to Prague. While enjoying a dainty snack the pretty stewardess leaned over our seat and asked, "Did you feel the jolt?" We looked up, our faces puzzled. She smiled and exclaimed, "No? But we just crashed through the Iron Curtain!"

Elaborate plans had been made for the climax of our visit. Charles University, founded one hundred years before Columbus "discovered" America, was to confer their highest honorary degree on my husband. No white American university had ever recognized that he had any claim to scholarship. He had earned three degrees from Harvard University. His Ph.D thesis, *The Suppression of the African Slave Trade*, published in 1896, had immediately been made Volume I in the Harvard Historical Series. Yet that university had never invited him there even to deliver a lecture, much less to receive any honor. And in New York, a white Harvard alumnus was prevented from taking Du Bois to the Harvard Club for lunch. Now, here was a famous old university thousands of miles from home anxious to honor him.

We interrupted our visit to Prague briefly to attend The First Conference of African and Asian Writers. It was held in Tashkent, the capital of Uzbekistan, the farthest south of the sixteen Republics of the Soviet Union. It is northeast of the continent of Africa, about center of the continents of Europe and Asia. The ancient city had been selected as the site for the conference which was seen as a continuation of the purpose which had inspired the Bandung Conference and was accelerated by the meeting of writers in Delhi in 1956. Forty-eight countries sent 168 representatives; those from the Asian republics of the Soviet Union brought the number to over two hundred. Uganda, Somaliland, Nigeria, Jordan and Palestine were represented by expatriates at present living in Cairo; Turkey was represented by its best loved poet, the exiled Nazim Hikmet. In addition there were at least a hundred writers from western Europe.

The impact of this assembly upon Du Bois cannot be overemphasized. Cedric Belfrage, founding editor of the *National Guardian*, described an exciting moment:

> The life of W. E. B. Du Bois received a crown of tribute in history's first gathering of writers from all Asia and Africa. With only his wife and one deported editor (Belfrage, himself) to record the occasion for his country's open press, the 90-year-old American scholar drew the only standing ovation to an individual in Tashkent's magnificent Maoit Theatre. . . . His voice rang clear from wall to intricately carved wall of the auditorium, speaking for the freer, friendlier, brinkless America for which he and his ancestors fought.

116

Attending the first Afro-Asian Writers conference, Tashkent, USSR, October, 1958. Above, Effie Sutherland, head of the Ghanaian delegation addressing Conference. Below, Du Bois meeting delegates at Tashkent Conference.

The closing hours of the conference were dramatized by the unanimous adoption of the *Appeal to the Writers of the World*, which called upon them "to raise your voices against all evils which are being committed both against individuals and against whole nations."

Speaking as the leader of the delegation from Ghana, the youngest nation in that body of many nations, was Effie Sutherland, who thanked the people of Tashkent for their warm and tireless hospitality and in the name of the African-Asian Conference of Writers pledged all to the unfaltering fulfillment of peace, friendship, and freedom. As she spoke, this statuesque black woman, her tall figure draped in the colors of her country's flag, green and red, with a headdress, like a crown, of the same colors, her eyes flashing in the deep-carved ebony of her face, she was Africa the Mother, Africa of deep and mighty rivers; Africa hailing the new dawn with joy and determination.

We returned to Prague, exhausted but inspired.

The ceremony of October 23 was a state affair. Engraved invitations had been sent out to all embassies and state officials. Before I was escorted to my place in the domed chambers, diplomats, foreign visitors, and friends filled the auditorium. Then from high overhead came a fanfare of trumpets, followed by music rolling from a great pipe organ. The audience rose to its feet and from the back, down the wide central aisle, marched a procession of medieval splendor, led by youths in scarlet and gold livery. Gorgeously clad professors and dons, men and women followed. And in the midst of all this pomp and circumstance, himself clothed in billowing robes and wearing an extremely chic black velvet hat, came the small, erect figure of W. E. B. Du Bois, to receive the degree of Doctor of the Science of History, *honoris causa.*

Conferring of the honorary degree at
Charles University, Prague, probably
the oldest university in the world.
Du Bois delivered his paper.

November 3 was a cold, clear morning in Berlin. Pale sunshine streamed through the high windows of the big university room. The faculty of Humbolt University, the Minister of Education, the Rector, and other officials and friends were awaiting our arrival. In one corner an ensemble played Bach chamber music. The low murmur of voices ceased when the Rector took his place at the podium and explained why the university was holding this special ceremony to bestow the degree of Doctor of Economics upon a scholar who had matriculated at the university in the past century.

"Records of this student's work have been preserved here. We have taken them out and carefully studied them. These records reveal the depth of this student's promise. Since that time . . ." And he outlined the distinctive achievements of W. E. B. Du Bois as scholar, educator, organizer, and champion of freedom, justice, and human dignity. "We therefore this morning honor our University and our State . . ." Du Bois accepted the scroll and responded, "Today you have fulfilled one of the highest ambitions of my young manhood." He paid tribute to the eminent men under whom he had studied in Berlin and closed with simple words of sincere thanks. After applause and hearty congratulations, the string ensemble played Bach and refreshments were served.

Conferring of degree at Humbolt University, formerly the University of Berlin.

We flew from Berlin on the morning of November 5, 1958, in order to be in the Soviet Union for the fortieth anniversary of the October Revolution. We were guests of the Soviet Peace Council and were cordially welcomed at the airport by Mikhail Kotov, Executive Secretary of the Council and a large delegation.

We were housed at the National Hotel on Sverdlov Square in old Moscow. I am sure the National Hotel dates from days long before the Revolution, and I have no doubt that princes, or at least high noblemen, more than once occupied the suite into which were were ushered. Its carpets, drapes, bed, pillows, covers, and heavy lace curtains were incredible. From its high windows it seemed to me I could see everything I had ever heard of Moscow. A short distance beyond the square was the Kremlin, and I could see a portion of its towers and buttresses from the window.

Warmer clothing was a necessity, since we planned to be out-of-doors a good deal, so one of my first chores was to shop for W. E. B. We bought a fur cap, fleece-lined boots, wool socks and wool underwear, to supplement his overcoat. I've been in crowds at Macy's in New York, but the crush of people at GUM, the large department store in Moscow, was worse.

Conference with Prime Minister Khrushchev in the Kremlin, January, 1959. It was a warm meeting on a very cold day.

The morning of the parade, November 7, was bright and cold. We were taken by our young guide and interpreter to our seats in the grandstand at Red Square. With the roar of a cannon, everyone was on his feet, cheering as forty mighty blasts of cannon fire greeted the fortieth anniversary of the October Revolution. The parade began.

After two or more hours, as the march continued, Du Bois complained of fatigue. I conveyed this to our interpreters and they called a guard, who secured an official to escort us from the grandstand. In skirting the side of the parade ground, we found ourselves directly in front of and below the elevated stand where Mr. Khrushchev stood, surrounded by all the top officials of the Soviet Union. Our official escort paused slightly and at that moment Mr. Khrushchev looked down and saw us. Du Bois turned to face him, whipped off his hat and gravely bowed. Mr. Khrushchev smiled, took off his hat and returned the bow. At this, everyone who had seen the exchange applauded. They could not have known who the dark little man was who received this attention, but they were certain he was *somebody*. Returning to our hotel, we watched the rest of the parade from the windows of our rooms.

In addition to sightseeing and being tourists, visiting the famed Bolshoi Theatre and having the opportunity to see the incomparable Ulanova in *Swan Lake*, we were fortunate to be able to attend a meeting of the Soviet Writers Union and to talk with Dr. Ivan Potekhin, Head of African Research in the Soviet Institute of Oriental Studies. He was very interested in knowing the fate of the Pan-African Congress, and about the relations between Africans and people of African descent in America. He complained that he was not happy with the limitations of work on Africa alone in an Institute of Oriental Studies. He said, "Africa is not part of the Orient. It is a separate and complete continent. It is not fitting that our studies should be lumped together with those on the Orient." My husband agreed and outlined a proposal for an Institute of African Studies, which he agreed to present to Mr. Khrushchev himself, when they met in private conference in January.

During that meeting with Mr. Khrushchev, my husband laid his proposal before the Premier. Mr. Khrushchev listened attentively, then promised to take it under serious consideration. We were received in his Kremlin office and the meeting lasted nearly two hours. The following year, the Institute of African Studies opened in Moscow, with Dr. Ivan Potekhin, Director. Three years later, in 1962, we had the opportunity of visiting the Institute, where Du Bois was welcomed as its initiator.

We both went to Barvikha, a health spa and sanitorium, about forty kilometers outside Moscow, for a complete rest from our rigorous tour. Russian winter had come; all the land was covered with deep snow. Pine trees stood like giant pillars in a white temple, the hush being broken only by the sound of sleigh bells. The lake was frozen over, but the big house was warm and cozy. The quiet was positively delicious. I left W. E. B. at Barvikha while I took his place at the All-African People's Conference in Accra, Ghana in mid-December. I traveled with the Russian observer's delegation led by Dr. Potekhin.

I read his message to the First All-African People's conference in Accra, Ghana, December 9, 1958. It began:

> Fellow Africans: about 1735, my great-great-grandfather was kidnapped on this coast of West Africa and taken by the Dutch to the colony of New York in America, where he was sold in slavery. About the same time a French Huguenot, Jacques DuBois, migrated from France, and his great-grandson, born in the West Indies and with Negro blood, married the great-granddaughter of my black ancestor. I am the son of this couple, born in 1868, hence my French name and my African loyalty.

I was glad to be in Africa. I was sorry my husband could not be there but I knew his heart and mind were with me. I hurried back to Russia to join him for the next part of our adventure.

Our Russian sojourn ended, we went to China. The last two days and nights of January, 1959 we spent in Siberia, enroute to Peking from Moscow. The weather and engine trouble made our lay-over at Omsk necessary. W. E. B. hated delays of any kind, and we were due in Peking. I enjoyed our brief interlude. Our quarters were quite adequate, the food was good, and never had I seen such brilliant sun shining on endless expanses of pure snow. Drawing in deep breaths was like drinking chilled champagne. I did not realize how very cold it was until the morning we were leaving when, out in the snow, I touched an iron fence with my bare fingers. They stuck, and I pulled away, leaving patches of skin on the railing.

Du Bois and I arriving in Peking from Moscow, early February, 1959.

Flying for hours from Omsk, we saw nothing but snow and ice; then came mountains and deep crevices; then bare desert plains. Finally, we were told that we were flying over the Gobi Desert and after a while, we were over a spreading, rolling plain, with here and there wide patches of green. We landed in the middle of one of those green patches. We had reached Peking, capital of the country that was ancient when men in Saxony lived in caves, the country which had been devastated by invaders, but the country which was now recreating itself in a new image; we had come to the People's Republic of China.

126

We were welcomed by Premier Chou En-lai for private dinner in
his home February, 1959. The surroundings were exquisite. Below,
After dinner talk with Chou En-lai.

Our visit to China took place in the first quarter of 1959, when China
was a highly controversial subject. Our visit was from the first of February to the last of April. In the course of that time we covered areas from
Peking to Shanghai to Wuhan; we traveled up the Yangtze River to
Chungking, west by plane to Chengtu and farther west into Szechwan
province by car to visit minority groups near the borders of Tibet, then
back to Kwangtung and down to Canton. During our visit, my husband
celebrated his 91st birthday.

We were taken to the Peking Hotel, a favorite meeting place for for-
eigners during the old days of the 1930's. We remained there for a couple
of weeks, attending the Peking Opera, the theatre, and sightseeing in general. All I knew about China before I arrived was what I had read in the
Western press. I sent an article to the *Pittsburgh Courier* in which I said:

> "If there is one over-all impression I get from the crowds on the
> streets of Peking, in the schools, movies, theatres and in the parks,
> it is that they are happy and excited about what they are doing."

The plans for the celebration of W. E. B.'s birthday were extensive. It began, the evening before, with a dinner party at the home of Premier Chou En-lai in a setting of beautiful tapestries and carved teakwood screens. With the Premier and his wife were perhaps a half-dozen high officials. The dinner itself was a feast for the eyes as well as for the taste buds. This artistry in preparing and serving food was something new. I have never seen it equaled. We were regaled that evening with excellent food and conversation, for although Chou En-lai did not speak English, I learned later that he understood the language very well.

The next evening, following a visit to Peking University where W. E. B. delivered an address to faculty and students from all of the schools and colleges in the city, was the big banquet, later described in a Peking newspaper as "A gala Chinese-style party to celebrate the ninety-first birthday of Dr. W. E. B. Du Bois, the famous American scholar and Negro leader." The top floor of the Peking Hotel had been converted into a temple hall with scrolls covered with traditional symbols of longevity decorating the walls, candles and flowers and miniature cypress trees on ceremonial tables, a huge birthday cake, and a bowl of "long-life" peaches from Premier Chou En-lai.

Du Bois' 91st Birthday Banquet in Peking, February 23, 1959. We were overwhelmed by the warmth of our reception.

While we ate dainty morsels of food, dancers and singers provided entertainment. Birthday messages were read, beginning with one from Mao Tse-tung and including greetings from the Soviet Union, the United States and other lands.

When the party was over we were assisted to our rooms, loaded down with presents; embroidered tapestries, a priceless piece of pottery from the Ming tombs, poems written on bamboo scrolls, eulogizing Du Bois, paintings, and books, among the last a copy of his *In Battle for Peace* in Chinese.

It was a birthday neither of us would forget.

One evening, during early spring, we were sitting on our vine-covered porch hearing the story of a picturesque pagoda on a hill on the other side of the lake. The setting sun now bathed it in beauty. It had been built several hundred years ago in memory of a poet who had immortalized the loveliness of this region. Dr. Ting Hsi-lin gave us the news that the next day, we would visit the leader of China's millions, Mao Tse-tung.

The next morning we went for the hour's drive to the place where Mao Tse-tung was resting, for our visit. The spring morning was a delight. A slight haze shot with gold hung over the land. In the fields plants were pushing up through the black soil, trees were delicately traced with young leaves and the light fresh breezes brought us the fragrance of fruit blossoms and spring flowers. Our car turned into a garden, and there on the porch of an attractive, low cottage stood the Wise Old Man of China.

A large man, Mao Tse-tung carried himself with military precision. But it was something other than his size that made him so impressive—something hard to define—but certainly there. Our visit extended through the afternoon. It was in no sense formal, rather very warm and friendly. His interpreter, a handsome young man, translated with such ease and fluency that there seemed no interruption in the conversation, to which we all contributed.

Later, we gathered around a table for discussion. Du Bois asked many questions which were answered fully and explicitly. I said nothing, but busily wrote in my notebook. It was while Chairman Mao was asking searching questions about the United States that Du Bois spoke of mistakes he had made in trying to carry forward his work. He spoke of several failures and how he regretted them. The Wise Old Man shook his head.

130

With us are Tang Ming-chao, now one of the Under-Secretaries of the United Nations, Ting-Hsi-lin, Vice-Chairman of the Chinese People's Association for Cultural Relations, Chu Po-shen, direct descendant of the last Chinese emperors, Anna Louise Strong, American writer who lived in China for many years, and our vivacious, fluent interpreters.

The only deplorable mistake a man makes is when he lies down and lets the enemy walk over him. This, I gather, you have never done. You have continued the struggle for your people, for all the decent people of America. Mistakes!" He spat out the word, leaned forward and his lips twisted in a wry smile. "The Communist Party of China has made all the mistakes there are to make! How many times were our armies forced to retreat? How many times have we had to change our course? But we never give up! Mistakes are but stepping stones upon which one may climb higher and higher—until finally from your elevated place you may look back and direct the way of those who came behind.

The sun lay in long slants across the land when we departed. Mao Tse-tung placed in my husband's hands a slender volume of his poems. All the remaining days of his life, this little book lay on the night table beside his bed, for early or late reading. As I looked into the expressive face of that leader who is regarded by his people with such affection and confidence, I knew I was in the presence of one of the world's truly great men.

We traveled through southern China before returning to Peking and were notified that the Soviet Union had conferred the Lenin Peace Prize on Du Bois. He was asked to be in Moscow for the May 1 celebrations. Shortly before leaving China we visited the grave of Agnes Smedley, an American writer who gave her life in the cause of oppressed peoples. We were accompanied by a group of American friends.

Our last days in China were so hectic. I never did get to the Great Wall which Du Bois had visited on a previous trip. We left Peking early on the morning of April 29 and set down at Moscow's airport shortly after dark. There had been one short stop at Omsk for refueling, and because we were flying eastward, the sun hovered on the horizon for hours.

May Day was a gala day in Moscow, with another long parade. This time the emphasis was on flowers and not on guns. Du Bois' picture was on the front pages of all the papers with the announcement of his Lenin Peace Prize.

Viewing the May 1 parade in Moscow's Red Square.

A week later we flew to Stockholm to attend the tenth anniversary of the World Peace Council. Though he had been elected one of its vice-presidents at Paris in 1949, because his passport had been withdrawn, Du Bois had been unable to attend any of its annual meetings. As soon as the conference was over we flew on to London. A very special treat awaited us there.

I sent a dispatch to the Pittsburgh Courier (on June 10, 1959). I said,

We have just returned to London after being guests of the Robesons in Stratford-on-Avon. And so we have been privileged to share in making history. I think Shakespeare would have been intrigued. Not since the beginning of the Shakespeare Memorial Theatre has the entire run of one play been sold out within the first week of its performance. The last performance of *Othello* will be in November. A railway switchman leaned through the window of our train compartment to tell us, "England will never find another Othello equal to Mr. Robeson." True, this switchman would hardly qualify as an expert on Shakespeare, but since April this switchman at Leamington Spa has witnessed a transformation in the old Shakespeare country. Trains, buses, automobiles, planes and boats are bringing people to Stratford-on-Avon from far and near . . . eager to "queue up" to see Paul Robeson. Standing room is sold for each performance for the capacity of the theatre. And unless you secured your tickets long ago, or are one of those fortunate souls who has a friend inside some magic circle, standing room is all you are going to get. . . . Being starred in the 100th Anniversary performance of Shakespeare Memorial Theatre is tops for any actor. . . . And how magnificently Paul fills the role! His presence is compelling, his voice runs the scale of human emotions, his eyes melt the heart one moment and flash with passion the next. . . . Beyond all question, here in his sixty-first year, Paul has given his best performance.

Behind stardom in Shakespeare Memorial Theatre lies the prestige of the British Empire—and herein lies the historical significance now being highlighted in Stratford-on-Avon. For Paul Robeson embodies in his person seething, erupting Africa, his voice carries the overtones of America's Negro spiritual, the poetry of his soul has been enriched by Pushkin, within his soul is blended the song of the Volga boatman and the Mississippi dock worker. After eleven months of travel, our night in Stratford-on-Avon was the perfect climax, the rounding-off pinnacle, the arrow pointing home.

We'll be home to celebrate the 4th of July in our own back-yard. Independence Day, Brother, and I mean INDEPEN-DENCE!

Paul standing in front of the Ann Hathaway cottage, where as Paul's guests we had spent the night, June, 1959.

Part Ten

WE spent a year at home in Brooklyn.

Du Bois had given up his downtown office, and during these months worked with a secretary on the last of his "Black Flame" trilogy and his "Soliloquy." Then in May, 1960 came the invitation to attend the founding of the Republic of Ghana and the inauguration of Kwame Nkrumah as Ghana's first President. At first there were some passport difficulties, but the Ghanaian ambassador straightened it out for us.

We arrived in Ghana, July 2, 1960. The heavy rainy season had just ended, and all the fresh-washed land was lush and green. We were housed in the spacious home of Justice Van Lare, and a car with driver was placed at our disposal. The inaugural ceremony on the morning of July 4 was a blending of African traditional ritual with the pomp and show of crowning a British king. Nkrumah, the man chosen by the people of the new Republic of Ghana to be their first president, stood before the closed doors of the first assemblage of Ghana's parliament. He lifted a golden chalice and poured fresh water from the Volta River before the door; then, speaking in a language which was old when Homer wrote, he prayed to Ghana's spiritual ancestors for protection and guidance and he thanked them for Ghana's "New Day."

Ceremony inside Parliament House.

As the great carved doors swung open, with drum beat and the trumpeting of the ram's horn, the procession marched solemnly down the central aisle. For the first time all officials were clothed in the kente cloth of their forefathers, wore sandals on their feet, and hung pure gold, dug from their soil, on themselves.

Following the official festivities, we set out to see Ghana, beginning in Accra, then traveling by car through the countryside, spending several days in Kumasi and at the Cape Coast. Upon our return to Accra, we were honored to have President Nkrumah as our dinner guest.

He had called to say that he wanted "to spend a long undisturbed evening with our Dear Doctor." That evening he talked of Ghana and its people, his hopes and plans for the future . . . he had confidence that Ghanaians would unite, work and accomplish much. He told us,

> "I have repeatedly said that this country and nation is not free so long as any part of our continent is enslaved." He leaned forward. "You, Doctor, inculcated into our souls the necessity of Pan-Africa—a united Africa. When I opened the All-African Peoples' Conference, here in Accra, to which your good wife so eloquently presented your address, I told them that this was in fact the Sixth Pan-African Congress as organized by you. I reminded them how colonial masters prevented you from holding such a conference on the continent of Africa; how you persevered, managed to get us together in different parts of Europe; how you injected us with confidence and hope until this day came when independent Ghana could assemble African peoples for a conference to consider their destiny. . . . And now, Doctor, I need your help."

Entering hall for dinner given by Ghana's Academy of Science, Accra.

It was then that Kwame Nkrumah approached my husband with the request that he come to Ghana to plan, set up and organize an *Encyclopedia Africana*. They talked further, Du Bois pointing out the scope and magnitude of the project and the time needed for outlining the work and his advanced age. Nkrumah waved aside his objections and secured from him the promise to "think it over." And, of course, he did.

Reception that evening following Inauguration.

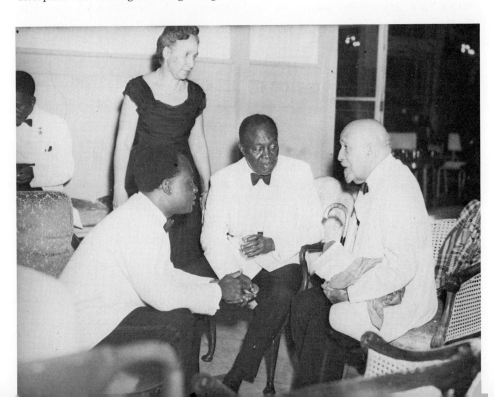

Contrary to reports that Du Bois had turned his back on the race, he remained active speaking on Black College campuses and at numerous conferences and institutes sponsored by Black scholars and educators. Here in April, 1960 at Johnson C. Smith College, we are with old and dear friend Dr. Helen G. Edmonds, author and historian, from North Carolina State College at Durham, N.C.

Part Eleven

BY the time we returned to Brooklyn Heights, Du Bois had decided to accept Nkrumah's offer. "We will move to Ghana where I'll spend the remainder of my days on this work. It could be the crowning undertaking of my life; gathering and recording true facts about the continent and peoples who have been so misrepresented to the world."

We returned home on the first of September. Yolande came up from Baltimore for a short visit. We couldn't know that it would be her last.

Du Bois, excited about the Encyclopedia project was already sending out letters to scholars and research bodies throughout the world. He told me, "The first duty of any researcher is not to jump at conclusions. I do not know what the reactions of any person on that list will be. And Shirley, if I undertake to build an *Encyclopedia Africana*, I shall proceed with the idea of gathering *all-true facts*—from whatever source they may come. It will be our job to sort out the false from the true, but we shall not proceed on a basis of unauthenticated legends or wishful thinking. I firmly believe that the continent of Africa, its history and its people can stand firmly and unafraid on the unvarnished, unembellished truth."

And so, behind the closed doors of his library, he and his secretary worked long hours, and sent out batches of letters daily to the post office. In the midst of this activity, the emblem-embossed invitation arrived inviting us to the inauguration of His Excellency Dr. Nnamdi Azikiwe as Governor-General and Commander-in-Chief of the Federation of Nigeria, 16 November, 1960. Du Bois observed, "I am not sure that this isn't a move to kick Azikiwe upstairs. He'd have remained closer to his people as prime minister than as representative of the Queen." He decided at once that we would go, since he had known Dr. Azikiwe for many years. He also wanted to talk over the encyclopedia with Dr. Kenneth Dike, head of Ibadan University in Nigeria and a recognized African scholar.

We landed in Lagos the second week in November and were promptly whisked off to the Federal Palace Hotel, situated on an island surrounded by its own lagoon and exuding an air of southern continental elegance. But during the first evening of our stay, an incident took place which was definitely African.

We had just seated ourselves in the glass-enclosed dining room overlooking the water. Bright tropical flowers added splashes of color where silver and glass gleamed on white oval tables. From the patio outside could be heard pleasant background sounds, music and conversation. Suddenly the big doors were flung open and into the room stalked a figure which might have just descended from Mount Olympus—a towering Black Zeus, quite capable of hurling thunderbolts. His voluminous white robe swirled about him in billows. In the same instant the air reverberated with a sound, not a whistle, not a call. It rose to a crescendo, then was sharply cut off by beating feet: "Z-E-E-E-E-E-E-K!" (Beat—beat.) It came from the waiters who stood motionless as the majestic figure bore down upon our table. Du Bois stood up and was enveloped in the billowing folds as the booming voice exclaimed, "Doctor, you're here—you're here! We are so glad—so glad!"

The Governor-General-elect explained that he was on his way to some function when he heard that Du Bois had arrived. "We had to stop and welcome you and your wife to our land—which is your land. After all the big doings are over, we'll have some long talks. You are our Father. Your sons in Africa cherish your advice."

Waving then to the other guests and with another "Z-e-e-e-e-k" he was gone.

The inaugural ceremonies with state dinner, luncheons, cocktail parties and a formal dance, were impressive. Dr. Azikiwe had invited his entire graduating class from Lincoln University in Pennsylvania to attend. Poet-novelist-playwright Langston Hughes was in that group, having a wonderful time.

Top left, R. Sargent Shriver, and W. E. B. Top right, Dr. Nnamdi Azikiwe, Governor-General of the Federation of Nigeria.

For three weeks we traveled about Nigeria; flew to Enuge, capital of Eastern Nigeria; from the chief river port Onitsha, we embarked for a trip on the Niger River, so wide in some places that one cannot see from bank to bank. Europeans were sinking oil wells near Port Harcourt—the forecast was of rich oil wells there. We visited Dr. Kenneth Dike, President of Ibadan University, with whom Du Bois discussed President Nkrumah's urgent demand that he undertake the setting up of an *Encyclopedia Africana.* Du Bois argued that he was too old to begin such an important project. Dr. Dike replied, "But you are the only man alive who can adequately present such a plan to all Africa; you are the Father of Pan-Africanism; you will get all our cooperation." (It is sad to think how much the bloody civil war has ravaged the country we saw in 1960. Rich oil fields have been found, but the masses of Nigerians still exist in poverty.)

Independence ceremony
in Nigeria, October, 1960.

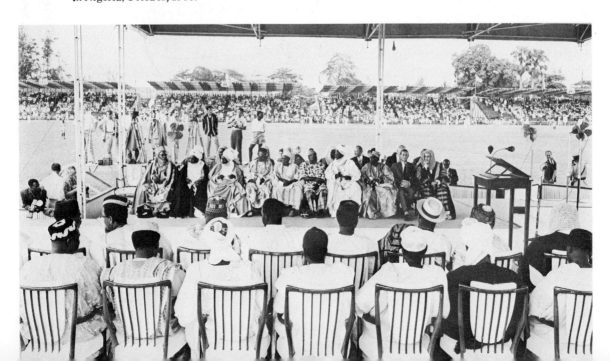

Now anxious to return home, we did not make any stops enroute to the United States. That first evening he telephoned Yolande in Baltimore, as he always did on returning from a long trip. She was happy to hear his voice, reported she was well and asked for details of the inaugural. He gave her some highlights, then said, "Shirley'll have to fill you in on all details when you come up for Christmas."

I heard Yolande's silvery laugh. She assured him she would be up as soon as her school was out for the holidays. He hung up with a happy smile on his face.

He then threw himself into the stacks of waiting mail, most of which were responses concerning the encyclopedia.

Then one morning I received a telephone call from Baltimore telling me that Yolande had had a heart attack and had died on the way to the hospital! "Dear God!" I thought, distracted. "This will kill him!"

It was a terrible shock. I tried to protect him, but I had to see my poor husband shrink to half his size. There was no defense against his grief, no consolation. "Why?" he asked me. "I am old; Yolande had so much life before her. Why should she go and I remain?" He lay on his bed, not weeping, but shaken by shudders which racked his body. After a while he told me, "She must be buried in Great Barrington beside her mother and the little boy. Phone them, Shirley."

Everything Du Bois wished was carried out and the hour came when, in the small, snow-covered New England cemetery, under dark, wintry skies, we stood beside the open grave and saw Yolande's coffin lowered into the frozen earth. Nothing could have been more bleak and desolate.

We did not have our usual Christmas at home or the traditional New Year's Open House. Du Bois went back to work on the Encyclopedia and I started working on a magazine project encompassing the freedom movement. The initiating group chose me as editor. The magazine was titled, *Freedomways.*

Now Du Bois had written President Nkrumah that he would come to Ghana to supervise the building of an *Encyclopedia Africana.* He was corresponding with Fisk University about sending them the greater portion of his large collection of books; he advised that we would sell the house. "I am too old," he told me, "to think about this as anything but a final move."

He was having some prostate problems and his doctor had fitted him with a supporting brace, which relieved discomfort, but still concerned me. An invitation to Rumania provided an opportunity for him to spend some time in Bucharest's *Institutue de Geriatrie,* where Dr. Anna Aslan had urged him to come during her visit to the United States. I knew he needed the rest and change of pace, so I urged him to go without me. Everything went without a hitch, or so it seemed.

Du Bois returned home from Rumania the latter part of July, refreshed, brisk and in excellent spirits. Meeting him at the airport, we saw him come in with other landing passengers. He looked up at us and waved. Then he disappeared from view in the line at the inspection desk. We hurried downstairs to await him at the exit gates. We waited for two hours. Inquiries only brought information that he was inside with the customs inspectors. When he did appear, we learned that he had been searched thoroughly, every line and every scrap of paper in his bags read, and he had been subjected to a barrage of questions. He told us, "The one in charge, who was excessively polite and apologized for the delay, spoke once in German and seemed amazed when I responded in kind. From then on he addressed me exclusively in German and concluded by treating me as if I were a fellow Nazi. He barked sharp orders and saw to it that everything was carefully and neatly put back into the bags."

Yolande came up from Baltimore for a short visit and we have here her last picture, taken with her father and his great-grandson, Arthur McFarlane, son of Yolande's daughter, Mrs. Du Bois Williams McFarlane. They are standing in front of our Brooklyn home. W. E. B. has wrapped about him the Ghanaian Kente cloth, gift from President Nkrumah.

I was furious. In the car, on the way home, he put his arms around me and murmured, "Stop worrying, darling. I haven't been harmed. Such things happen in a police state. This is a fact we have to face."

We attended a cocktail party a couple of weeks later at the home of one of the UN ambassadors. These affairs always brought together a stimulating and varied group of people. I found myself being drawn aside by a Washington lawyer whom I knew very well. He said, "I've heard the Doctor is seriously considering going to Ghana to undertake a project with Nkrumah. When does he plan to go?"

"No set time, but probably early spring," I replied. "He must consider it important," he stated.

"Indeed! He considers it the crowning undertaking of his life."

"Then," he said, casting a quick look around and with lowered voice, "he must get out of here before October 9!" I stifled a cry of surprise, but before I could say a word he continued. "That day, the U.S. Supreme Court is going to hand down an adverse opinion on the Communist Party and Dr. Du Bois will most certainly be one of the citizens of this country who will be prevented from travelling anywhere."

Before I could ask questions, he smiled, but said earnestly, "Tell him!" and casually walked away.

Upon hearing the news, Du Bois exploded. "They shall not stop me. I'll not be chained up here! We'll go—we'll go quickly!"

We now had six weeks to do everything we had planned for six months.

For a long time there had been a tacit agreement that Herbert Aptheker would someday edit Du Bois' letters, it being understood that I would write the biography, which together would comprise the life and letters of W. E. B. Du Bois. Du Bois told Herbert, "It will be an enormous job to pull out the books and papers we must take with us (those relating to Africa, Pan-Africanism and personal papers, he had decreed must go to Africa). I'm sending the major portion of my library to Fisk, but the files will have to be handled separately." "We'll do it," Aptheker agreed, and the next day he was on hand to work.

Breaking up a home is always sad. We had made a good home at 31 Grace Court, one in which we had been very happy. W. E. B. wandered through the rooms as they were being dismantled, his eyes glazed. I know now, better than I did then, how deeply he felt the wrench. Moreover, there was something akin to flight in the precipitous manner of our going, which was repugnant to him. This was his home and although work called him elsewhere, he did not want to feel forced to leave it.

146

Here we are leaving for Ghana at the New York airport, 1961; W. E. B.'s cousin, Mrs. Alice Crawford, with his great-grandson, Arthur McFarlane. We knew he would never return to the U.S. Below, the Ghanaian Ambassador giving autographs.

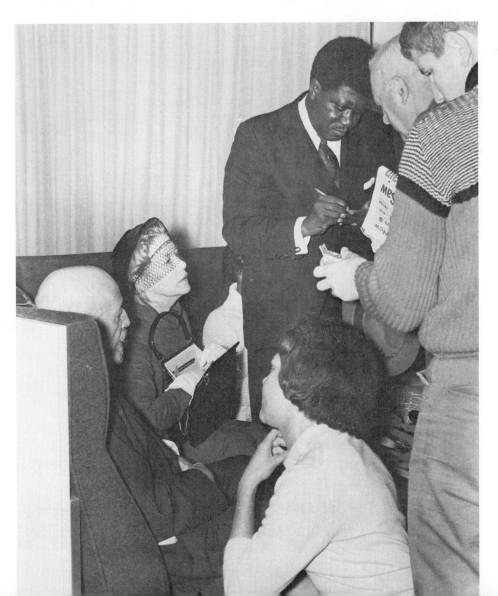

I am certain it was out of this feeling of pride, mingled with hurt, that he reached another decision, a decision declaring his independence. He showed me the letter several days before mailing it—the letter which may be read in full in *His Day Is Marching On.*

It was to Gus Hall, Chairman of the Communist Party of the U.S.A. In the letter Du Bois said, "On this first day of October, 1961, I am applying for membership in the Communist Party of the United States. I have been long and slow in coming to this conclusion, but at last my mind is settled."

He then reviewed his knowledge and exposure to Communist doctrine from his college days in Berlin, his introduction to the Socialist Party, and his work with the NAACP, his path up to and including the Cold War and the Progressive Movement. He ended his letter by enumerating ten demands that he would call for as a member of the American Communist Party, which he said, "will provide the United States with a real Third Party, and thus restore democracy to this land."

1. Public ownership of natural resources and of all capital.
2. Public ownership of transportation and communications.
3. Abolition of poverty and limitation of personal income.
4. No exploitation of labor.
5. Social medicine, with hospitalization and care of the old.
6. Free education for all.
7. Training for jobs and jobs for all.
8. Discipline for growth and reform.
9. Freedom under law.
10. No dogmatic religion.

These aims are not crimes. They are practiced increasingly over the world. No nation can call itself free which does not allow its citizens to work for these ends.
(signed)
W. E. B. Du BOIS

Although everybody agreed with us that any "demonstration" was undesirable, there must have been two hundred people at the airport the night of our departure. This included several Ghanaian officials, reporters and cameramen, a half-dozen lawyers and a host of warm and faithful relatives and friends who, though anxious and unhappy, were determined to send 'Dr. Du Bois away with a smile.' The moment came. Standing at the top of the steps leading into the plane, Du Bois waved gaily to the crowd. After that he never looked back.

On the 9th of October 1961 the U.S. Supreme Court handed down a decision which deprived thousands of the citizens of the United States of basic and fundamental civil rights.

Part Twelve

I had written ahead that we wanted to buy a house in Ghana, stating that we would prefer an old house in a garden. It seemed such a place had been found. It stood on a hill, at a crossroads, in the middle of an acre of ground and surrounded by high hedges. On each side of the main entrance stood umbrella-like flamingo trees, green now, which in season would be red. There were many trees, here and there were giant ferns, their graceful, feathery fronds waving gently. The kitchen was separate from the house but connected by a roofed walk. Over the kitchen a tall paw paw tree leaned, heavy with golden melons. Beyond it I saw a mushroom shaped banana tree. Tall, willowy shoots screened a small building in one corner designated as the servant's quarters.

Inside the house were five rooms, each finished with fine hardwood. We would need more library space and I immediately suggested the addition of a large room, with bath, in the front and open to breezes from three sides. This would be W. E. B.'s bedroom, well removed from the rest of the house. As I walked about I could see it as it would be: a big, sprawling, comfortable home with screened porch and lots of windows, shaded by trees. Orchids would bloom in our garden, and in the evening glistening water from sprinklers would spray the lawns and the twilight would be filled with the fragrance of orange and lemon blossoms, jasmine and honeysuckle.

And that is the way it was.

Du Bois had decided that he wanted Dr. Alphaeus Hunton, former colleague in the Council on African Affairs, as his chief assistant on the encyclopedia. Dr. Hunton was then teaching in Guinea. It was suggested that he be invited to Ghana to discuss the possibility. Dr. Hunton came and said that he would gladly join this project if he could be relieved of his duties in Guinea without too much difficulty. Because of the importance of the encyclopedia, Nkrumah promised personally to take up the matter with President Sekou Toure.

The New Year came in with very good promise—and then the old prostate trouble recurred. Dr. Aslan, on a visit to Ghana, advised Du Bois to return with her to Bucharest. He laughed and said he couldn't spend his time being "pampered." Dr. Hunton was scheduled to join him by the end of March, and it looked as though by spring, the Secretariat, with full staff, would be set up in its own offices.

The first Sunday in February we went to visit an Afro-American friend who was teaching at a girls' boarding school in Aburi. It was about an hour's drive and the day was hot. Before we reached our destination, W. E. B. told me he was in pain. As soon as we arrived I had him lie down. I stayed with him until he said the pain had eased and insisted on getting up. He went to the luncheon table, but did little more than toy with his food. During the trip back it was cooler and we arrived home without mishap, but during the night he became feverish and I saw that he was suffering. He would not let me call the doctor, insisting that the next morning we would go directly to the hospital, where "he has facilities for a thorough examination and there are other doctors for consultation," he said. I knew then that he thought something serious was the matter.

I have tried to banish the next days from my mind; the memory of what he suffered is almost more than I can bear. And I am convinced an operation two years earlier would have removed the cause. The gland, now enlarged and inflamed, was sending poison throughout his system and was about to burst. It had to be punctured immediately. He could not be moved. Should the gland burst he would die. The next several days were terrible. On the third day, I was able to take him home from the hospital, which was little more than a clinic, on a stretcher. We had prepared his room with sterile equipment and had two nurses and a steward to assist with his care.

Gradually the poison drained away and some color returned to his face. But it was only a temporary relief; the cause of the trouble remained. I sent off a letter to Dr. Aslan. She cabled back to bring him to Bucharest as soon as his strength permitted. If an operation was necessary, she said in a follow-up letter, a specialist would be brought from Moscow to perform it. That is how my husband spent his 94th birthday flying over the Alps to Rumania.

W. E. B.'s Ghanaian nurse.

Breakfasting on our cheerful sun porch in our new home.

Ten days later, the Russian specialist, with assistant and interpreter arrived from Moscow. At the end of another week of examinations and tests, I was called in for a conference with the doctors. They gave me lengthy details on W. E. B.'s condition. The immediate solution was extremely complicated. His age presented uncalculable risks. It added up to the decision not to operate. Dr. Pytel, a large, good-natured man with a decided air of authority, offered a solution, in the form of a surgical appliance that would allow the gland to remain open, while cutting off seepage to other parts of the body. The appliance would have to be worn at all times. "Will he be well?" I asked, doubtfully.

"He will recover his normal strength and well-being. But you must remember, madam, your husband is ninety-four years old. It is only natural that his general vitality should diminish." He added, "We are not going to tell him that an operation is impossible, but only that he must become stronger, and that we will look in on him again in three or four months."

The appliance had to be made on specifications in London and in due course it arrived. I was instructed how to maintain its sterile condition and after his initial withdrawal and dismay, Du Bois accepted the doctors' assurances that this was a necessary inconvenience that must be borne for a short time. Now he could move about more freely.

We returned to Accra by way of Cairo, where my son David was with an Egyptian news agency. W. E. B. had never seen that city and David met us with a car at the airport. He took us to the new Shepheard's Hotel, where the balcony of our room on the seventh floor overlooked the Nile. After a good night's sleep David drove us out to the pyramids. We did not get out of the car, but drove slowly through the sands of Giza so that W. E. B. could get the best possible views, then swooped down upon the Sphinx. That evening the Chinese ambassador had us to dinner. The next day we left Cairo airport on a Ghana Airline plane and within a matter of hours were "at home" in Accra. Our home was now really in Africa.

Headquarters for the encyclopedia Secretariat was only a pleasant drive from our house, and a week after our return Du Bois was in his office drawing up plans for a monthly information bulletin. He allowed no abridgment of the Secretariat's authority and found it necessary to write Professor Boateng of the Ghana Academy of Sciences, regarding the use of the word, "Project" instead of "Secretariat," in several writings regarding the encyclopedia. Wrote Du Bois in his typical manner, "I do not like the change and will not accept such a position."

Du Bois was not reconciled to his apparatus. "He was bitter when Dr. Pytel explained that he would have to wait at least a year before they would consider operating." That means I'm to remain trussed up like this for the rest of my life. Let me die now!" He turned his face to the wall and refused to eat. Nkrumah knew what the doctors had told me in Bucharest. "We'll have to find someone who will operate. He must have this chance," I said, and Nkrumah came to see Du Bois and told him, "Cheer up, we'll find one who will take your case—don't *you* let us down."

Cables and telephone calls went out from Ghana; finally a telephone call came from Dr. Belfield-Clarke, Ghana's Chief Medical Officer. He was in London. A Trinidadan, he and Du Bois had been friends for forty years. Now he told me that he had found a man, tops in his field, but that we would have to bring Du Bois to London. I agreed without hesitation.

Eight days later, after exhaustive and strength-draining tests and examinations, Dr. D. R. Davies, the specialist, told me. "Your husband has a fifty-fifty chance to survive the operation. This is not as good as I had hoped. . . . I cannot make the decision to operate. You must do that. Think it over tonight. If you decide for the operation, I shall go ahead at once. Think it over."

I could not make the decision alone. Our lives were so closely knit that we must face this together. He held my hand tight while I told him. Then he looked at me, his eyes full of trust and love.

> "Shirley, you know I want to live. I have important work to do. But I do not want to drag on an increasingly helpless invalid. I want to be master of my own body. If there is *any* chance of me being freed from this accursed truss and restoring me to a reasonable amount of health, we must take it. *Tell the doctor to operate.*"

There were anxious days ahead, but on August 1, I was able to write David, "He is going to be well again." We went to Vevey in Switzerland for his recuperation and soon Du Bois was taking short walks and showing interest in the excellent food. In the middle of the second week, we had a telephone call from Charles Chaplin's secretary, indicating that Mr. Chaplin had been informed by a mutual friend that Dr. Du Bois was in Vevey recuperating from surgery and that if Dr. Du Bois was feeling well enough that Mr. Chaplin would like to send his car the following morning to bring Dr. Du Bois and his wife to spend some time in his home.

We were picked up by his car about eleven o'clock the next day, and after a short and pleasant drive were ushered into a large living room with lots of comfortable and much-used furniture. A fire glowed in the large fireplace. "Come sit by my fire, Doctor," said Chaplin as he led Du Bois to a deep and comfortable armchair. Du Bois stretched out his hands to the fire, as Mrs. Oona Chaplin and I made our way up to the second floor of the big, sunny house. The baby, their eighth child, was fast asleep in his crib, and two rosy-cheeked cherubs playing in the

On the terrace with an American couple who live in Peking.

nursery came forward and curtsied solemnly. They trailed after us as
we walked through the house and grounds and were delighted to pose
for pictures. Chaplin's older son Sidney, by a previous marriage, joined
us for lunch. A handsome man, with a thick mane of wavy hair and
brooding eyes, he was on a short visit with the family. We left later that
afternoon thinking, what a joy to be in a real home, bursting with love
and contentment.

We planned our trip back to Ghana by permitting the Chinese con-
sulate in Geneva to make all of the arrangements. It was planned as a
leisurely trip with one night of rest at Prague and two nights in Moscow.

We arrived in Peking in time for the thirteenth anniversary of the
People's Republic of China. We sat beside Chou En-lai at the banquet
given in the now-completed stately Great Hall of the People.

We were taken to a house in the suburbs, with nurse and doctor in
constant attendance. W. E. B. walked and sat in the gardens, sometimes
with friends who came out to drink tea and chat with him. The doctors
advised him, "Stay with us during the winter months. Your recovery is
remarkable, but you should give your system time to rebuild and restore
lost energy." "Delay your return," they urged. But he was feeling completely well and daily becoming more restless.

154

W. E. B. taking the sun in a park.

Then we were back in Accra with the hottest season drawing near. Du Bois threw himself into work. There was much to do. Du Bois set about planning a series of conferences in various parts of Africa. His idea was that these local conferences would stimulate interest and broaden the efforts of local research workers.

I am sure that the many signs of Ghana's growth and development and its forward-looking vision impelled my husband to become a Ghanaian citizen. President Nkrumah knew that it was a reaffirmation of Du Bois' faith and confidence in him and in Ghana's future. On February 15th when he received the Certificate of Naturalization, Du Bois wrote the Ghana Minister of Interior expressing his deep content and concluding:

My great-grandfather was carried away in chains from the Gulf of Guinea. I have returned that my dust shall mingle with the dust of my forefathers. There is not much time left for me. But now, my life will flow on in the vigorous young stream of Ghanaian life which lifts the African Personality to its proper place among men. And I shall not have lived and worked in vain.

155

It was a very hot afternoon when he received honorary degree from the University of Ghana; Vice-Chancellor Connor Cruse O'Brien, presiding. Invested with hood by Nana Nketsia, Ashanti Paramount Chief and Oxford scholar. Du Bois greets morning visitors with a happy smile and gives interviews.

A letter came from Nana Nketsia, Chairman of the Board of Trustees of the University of Ghana. It informed Du Bois that he had been nominated to receive the University's first honorary degree. The ceremony would be held on the university grounds, February 23, the anniversary of his birth.

Here we were at his 95th birthday, and he was not approaching it in as good a shape as I had hoped. He seemed to feel the heat much more than formerly. He was getting up very early, going to the office earlier and returning before noon in order to avoid the heat. His library at home had air-conditioning. Here he would often work after his return from the office. Yet he was losing the weight he had put on after the surgery, his appetite was uncertain and there were signs of diminishing strength. There was no recurrence of the old trouble, no pain or other evidences of illness. I redoubled my efforts to nourish him and tried to relieve him of work whenever I could.

I tried to bring as much pleasure into his life as was possible. So I was overjoyed when we received the news that Bernard Jaffe, one of the defense lawyers and our good friend, was coming for his birthday. We planned a double celebration: a birthday dinner for Du Bois and the President's wife Fatiha (her birthday is February 24). I planned to have a few friends in afterward to drink toasts to both birthdays, and then the Ghana security forces stepped in and I learned that Presidents are not "free."

It turned out that there could be no strangers or outsiders at the dinner-party. Connor Cruse O'Brien, the Head of the University of Ghana and his wife had been invited dinner guests. Now I had to ask Marge O'Brien if she would take over my house guest as well.

The morning of his ninety-fifth birthday, W. E. B. was awakened by the voices of school children singing in the garden. They came, bringing him flowers, and scarcely had he finished his breakfast when other visitors arrived: citizens, freedom fighters, and ambassadors and their wives bringing gifts. Sitting in his easy chair, he received them all. Journalists came and snapped pictures while he talked. His eyes were crinkling with mirth and his lips parted in a broad smile in one photograph which hangs above my desk.

Jaffe arrived in time for lunch and it was good to see and talk to him, again. In the afternoon, we drove to the University for the impressive ceremony.

That evening President and Mme. Nkrumah arrive for birthday dinner. Du Bois and I present Mme. Nkrumah with gift for her birthday, which is February 24. Cutting the birthday cake for W. E. B. and Mme. Nkrumah.

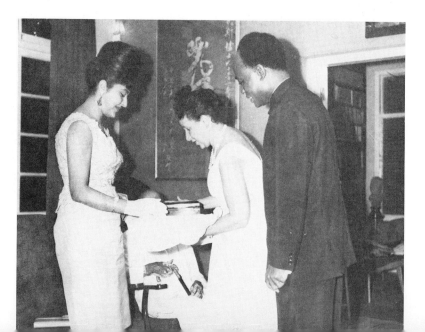

Later that evening the President and his wife arrived for dinner. It was a good day for W. E. B. His spirits were high and his voice buoyant.

After the guests had gone, I put on his favorite recording, the Ninth Symphony by Beethoven. He gave himself up to the music and started to sing. The ageless voice with its precise diction, rang clear and true.

Deine Zauber binden wieder,
Was die Mode streng geteilt:
Alle Menschen werden Burder,
Wo dein sanfter Flugel weilt.

On June 21, Du Bois attended the National Assembly when the President placed the Charter of African Unity before that body for ratification. Du Bois read with pride and satisfaction the many plans for its implementation.

The first week in July, Abbott Simon came for a visit with us. On the morning of July 4, we all drove to the Aburi Botanical Gardens, one of Du Bois' favorite drives. Simon was enchanted with everything he saw. I wanted to purchase a couple of orange trees from the Garden's nursery and I wanted a particular young tree that had attained some growth. The superintendent gave me special instructions for planting, after being assured that they were for "The good Doctor," and being taken to the car to meet Du Bois. That evening, shortly before sundown, we planted our orange trees. W. E. B. chose the spot. When I finished, W. E. B. reached for my hand.

"So," he said softly, "we are planting more trees, creating more solace and beauty. These trees, as the ones we planted in Brooklyn, will grow and flourish through the years." He smiled in happy anticipation.

Yet his strength was draining away. He began setting his papers in order, and he told me what he wanted done with the many unfinished pieces of work in the files.

President Ben Bella of Algeria came to Ghana, visited Du Bois and invited him to come to Algeria where he would get the salubrious breezes of the Mediterranean. He was our last major visitor.

On August 27, my dear husband, W. E. B. Du Bois, slipped peacefully away.

160

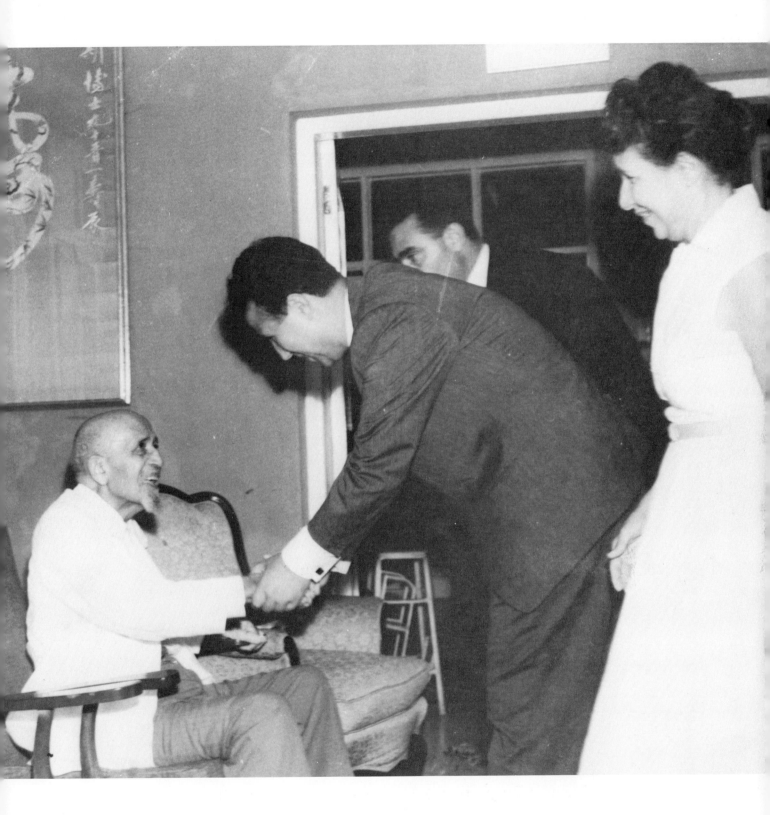

Nana Nketsia, paramount chief, poured libations to the gods of Africa before the casket was taken away from our home. I took a long last look before the casket was closed. President Nkrumah ordered a State funeral, which was held with full pomp and ceremony. Later a private memorial service was held with his favorite Beethoven played at the end.

Dr. WILLIAM EDWARD
DU BOIS.
BORN FEBRUARY 23RD 1868
AT GREAT BARRINGTON,
MASSACHUSETTS, U.S.A.
THE CHIEF JUSTICE
R.I.P.

Last Message

of Dr. Du Bois to the World

The body of Dr. W. E. B. Du Bois was laid to final rest with full military honours on the afternoon of August 29 at a spot some fifty yards from the pounding surf, beside the wall of The Castle, residence of the President of Ghana. Immediately following the interment, a last message to the world written by Dr. Du Bois was read to the thousands of assembled mourners. It was dated June 26, 1957, and had been given to me for safekeeping until the hour of his death.

This is the Message:

IT is much more difficult in theory than actually to say the last good-bye to one's loved ones and friends and to all the familiar things of this life.

I am going to take a long, deep and endless sleep. This is not a punishment but a privilege to which I have looked forward for years.

I have loved my work, I have loved people and my play, but always I have been uplifted by the thought that what I have done well will live long and justify my life; that what I have done ill or never finished can now be handed on to others for endless days to be finished, perhaps better than I could have done.

And that peace will be my applause.

One thing alone I charge you. As you live, believe in life! Always human beings will live and progress to greater, broader and fuller life.

The only possible death is to lose belief in this truth simply because the great end comes slowly, because time is long.

Good-bye.

Photographic Credits

Index

Hayes, Rutherford B., 13, 16
Herndon, A. F., 35
Hershaw, L. M., 35, 36, 37, 40
Hill, Richard, 35
His Day Is Marching On, 94, 148
Hope, John, 37, 67
Horizon, The (ed. Du Bois), 30, 40
Howard, Perry, Jr., 63
Howard University, 74
Howell, William, 63
Hughes, Langston, 63, 142
Humboldt University, Berlin, 120–121
  see also Friedrich Wilhelm University,
  Berlin
Hunton, W. Alphaeus, 63, 98, 150, 163
Hurst, John, 37

I

Institute of African Studies (Ghana), 154
Institute on African Studies (Moscow), 128
International Youth Festival, 84

J

Jackman, Harold, 63
Jackson, William T., 10
Jacklyn, Emily Basset, 6
Jaffe, Bernard, 157
James, William, 10, 12
Jefferson Davis (by W. E. B. Du Bois), 15
John Brown (by W. E. B. Du Bois), 36
Johnson, Charles S., 73
Johnson, James Weldon, 43, 50, 67, 71
Johnson, Mordecai W., 71
Johnson, W. B., 37
Johnson, W. D., 37
Jones, Eugene K., 71
Jones, Sidney, 105
Jourdain, E(dwin) B., 34

K

Kate Field's Washington (magazine), 14
Kritik der Reinen Vernunft (Emmanuel
  Kant's Critique of Pure Reason), 10
King, Charles A., 37
Krushchev, Nikita, 123–124
Ku Klux Klan, 47

L

Labor Party (N.Y.), 84
Lawson, Belford, 86
Leland, Waldo G., 71
Lenin Peace Prize, 132
Lewis, Sarah Marsh, 6
Lewis, William H., 12
Lincoln Institute (Mo.), 19
Lincoln's (A.), Tomb, 74
"Litany for Atlanta," 42
Lochard, Metz, 75, 105
Locke, Alain, 71
Loram, Charles T., 71
lynching, 40, 47–49, 51

M

McCard, Chita, 62
McCracken, Kathryn, 62
McFarlane, Arthur Edward II, 145, 153
  (W. E. B. Du Bois' great-grandson)
McGhee, P. L., 35, 37
McGhee, Ruth, 62
McGuire, Judge Matthew F., 90
Madden, James L., 35, 37
Mansart Trilogy, 98
Mao Tse-tung, 130–131
Marcantonio, Vito, 90
Marriage Among American Negroes, 57
Marsh, Clarence S., 71
Maynor, Dorothy, 74
Miller, Alex F., 63
Miller, Arthur, 88
Miller, George Frazier, 35, 37, 63
Mitchell, George W., 34, 37
Mitchell, O. L., 37
Monroe, F. S., 37
Moore, Fred R., 32
Moos, Elizabeth, 86, 90
Morgan, Clement G., 10, 13, 16, 35, 37, 38
Morris, E. T., 35
Morris, William, 11
Mundy, Alice, 62
Murphy, George, 84
Murray, F. H. M., 35, 36, 37, 40

N

Nail, Jack, 50
Napier, J. C., 32
National Association for the Advancement of
  Colored People (NAACP), 30, 42, 43,
  50, 51, 52, 54, 56, 77–78
National (Negro) Business League, 32
N.Y. Furriers Union, 92
Niagara Movement, 27, 34–39, 40, 42
Nigeria, Du Bois in, 146–147
Nketsia, Nana, 157, 164–165
Nkrumah, Fathia (Mrs. Kwame Nkrumah)
  158–159
Nkrumah, Kwame, 137–139, 141, 150, 155,
  158–159, 164–165

O

Oberlin College, 10
"Of Mr. Booker T. Washington and others,"
  27
O'Brien, Dr. and Mrs. Connor Cruse, 156–
  157
"On the Passing of the First Born," 26
Organization of African Unity, 154
Ovington, Mary White, 44

P

Pan-African Congress, 52–53, 56, 77
Paris Exposition (1900), 29
Paris Peace Conference, 81